This book is dedicated to Vicken, my inspiration and my strength.

Publisher's Acknowledgements
We would like to thank the following authors and publishers for their kind permission to reprint articles: **Art Gallery of New South Wales**; **Contemporary Sculpture Centre**, Tokyo; **Irish Museum of Modern Art**, Dublin; **Malmö Konsthall**; **Declan McGonagle**, Dublin; **Serpentine Gallery**, London; **Tate Gallery Liverpool**, and **Winnipeg Art Gallery**. We are grateful to the following for lending reproductions: **Chinati Foundation**, Marfa, Texas; **Paula Cooper Gallery**, New York; **Richard Deacon**, London; **Gateshead Metropolitan Council**, Tyne and Wear; **Anthony d'Offay Gallery**, London; **Feature Inc.**, New York; **Illuminations Television**, London; **Lisson Gallery**, London; **Louisiana Museum**, Humlebaek, Denmark; **PaceWildenstein**, New York; **Karsten Schubert Gallery**, London; **Bill Woodrow**, London; and **Donald Young Gallery**, Seattle. Photographers: **Isabelle Blondiau, Luis Bustamante, Boris Cvjetanovic, Chris Davies, Gautier Deblonde, Todd Eberle, John Kellett, Mary Kristen, Helmut Kunde, Reiner Lautwein, John McWilliams, Dag Mirostrand, Daro Montag, Andrew Moore, Sue Ormerod, Keith Pattison, Keith Paisley, Antonio Pinto, Saint Clair Cemin, David Scott, John Searle, Mariusz Szachowski, Jan Uvelius, David Ward, Boyd Webb, Stephen White, Alan Winn** and **Edward Woodman**. Special thanks are due to the White Cube Gallery, London, and to Claire Doherty and Clare Manchester for their assistance in the preparation of materials.

Artist's Acknowledgements
Thanks to my assistants, past and present: Steven Pippin, Ian Nutting, Tom Yuill, Niall O'Hare, Robert Turvey, Tim Maslen, Jonathan Lakin-Hall, Peter Moss, Carl Von Weiler, Pauline Woodrow, Victoria Putler, Laurence Kavanagh, Matthew Houlding, Tom Woolford, Dorian Hobday, Richard Galpin, Kenneth Kawamoto.

All at Thomas Clarke's and Hargreaves Foundries, and Malin Bridge and Copley Engineers.

Steve White and Gautier Deblonde for photography.

And special thanks to Margarida King for her help with compiling the additional material in this edition.

I would also like to thank Iwona Blazwick, who commissioned the first edition of this monograph, and Gilda Williams, Ian Farr, John Stack, Clare Stent, Veronica Price and Stuart Smith at Phaidon Press.

All works are in private collections unless otherwise stated.

Phaidon Press Limited
18 Regent's Wharf
All Saints Street
London N1 9PA

First published 1995
Second edition, revised and expanded, 2000
© 2000 Phaidon Press Limited
All works of Antony Gormley are © Antony Gormley.

ISBN 0 7148 3952 3

A CIP catalogue record of this book is available from the British Library.

Printed in Hong Kong

Design: SMITH

cover, **Another Place**
1997
Cast iron
100 figures, 189 × 53 × 29 cm each
Installation, Cuxhaven, Germany

page 4, **Sense** (detail)
1991
Concrete
74.5 × 62.5 × 60 cm

page 6, **Antony Gormley**
1990

page 30, **Lost Subject I,** in progress
1994

page 96, **European Field**
1994
Terracotta, approx. 35,000 figures
Variable size, each figure 8-26 cm
Installation, Muzej Surremene Umjetnosh, Zagreb

page 106, **Bodyprint in the Snow**
1979

page 164, background, **Another Place**
1997
Cast iron
100 figures, 189 × 53 × 29 cm each
Installation over 3 km², Cuxhaven, Germany

page 192, **Body,** in progress
1991

John Hutchinson E.H. Gombrich Lela B. Njatin W.J.T. Mitchell

Antony Gormley

Φ

Contents

Contents

E. H. Gombrich in conversation with **Antony Gormley**

Field for the British Isles (detail)
1992
Terracotta, approx. 35,000 figures
Variable size, 8-26 cm each
Collection, the Arts Council of Great Britain, London

Antony Gormley **You ought to know that it was reading *The Story of Art* at school that I think inspired my interest in art.**

Ernst Gombrich Really!

Gormley **… and made the whole possibility not only of studying art but also of becoming an artist a reality for me.**

Gombrich That's very flattering and very surprising for me.

Gormley **And what I hoped we might do in this conversation was talk about the relationship of contemporary art to art history generally – what is necessary, as it were, to retain and what we can discard from the lessons of that history.**

Gombrich I would like to start, like everybody else, with *Field*. I'm interested in the psychology of perception; if a face emerges from a shape you are bound to see an expression. The Swiss inventor of the comic strip, Rodolfe Toepffer, says that oddly enough, one can acquire the fundamentals of practical physiognomy without ever actually having studied the face, head or human contours, through scribbling eyes, ears, and nose. Even a recluse, if he's observant and persevering, could soon acquire – alone and with no help except what he gets from thousands of tries – all he needs to know about physiognomy in order to produce expressive faces. Wretched in their execution perhaps but definite and unmistakable in their meaning. He gives examples of doodles all of which have a strong expressive character. Anyone can discover in studying these doodles what makes for expression. I have called this 'Toepffer's law' – the discovery that expressiveness or physiognomy does not depend on observation or skill but on self-observation.

Gormley **For me the extraordinary thing about the genesis of form of the individual figures in *Field* is that it isn't about visual appearances at all. What I've encouraged people to do is to treat the clay almost as an extension of their own bodies. And this takes some time. This repeated act of taking a ball of clay, and using the space between the hands as a kind of matrix, as a kind of mould out of which the form arises.**

Gombrich Anyone who has ever played with clay has experienced this elemental form. And of course in twentieth century art, not only in your art, this played a crucial role. Picasso did it from morning to night, didn't he? He just toyed with what would come out when he created these shapes. When we loose the constraints of academic tradition we not only create an expressive physiognomy but an expressive shape or a more independent usage; that's what we admire in children's drawings, though I dare say that children do not intend to do so. We cannot help seeing the creations of primitive art in terms of an expressiveness, which is not always the one intended by the maker. In a certain frame of mind we see everything as expressive. The basis of our whole relationship to the world, as babies or as toddlers, is that we make no distinction between animated and inanimate things. They all speak to us, they all have a kind of character or voice. If you think back to your childhood, not only toys but most things which you encounter have this very strong character or physiognomy as Beings of some sort. And I'm sure that this is one of the roots or one of the discoveries of twentieth century art, to try to recapture this. In my view, it was too exciting to discover how creative and expressive the images made by children, the insane, and the untutored were. It's no wonder that artists longed to become like little children, to throw away the ballast of tradition that cramp their spontaneity and thus thwart their creativity. But it's no wonder also that new questions arose about the nature of art which were not so easily answered. Deprived of the armature of tradition and skill, art was in danger of collapsing into shapelessness. There were some who welcomed this collapse, the Dadaists and other varieties of anti-artists. But anti-artists only functioned as long as there was an art to rebel against, and this happy situation could hardly last. Whatever art may be, it cannot pursue a line of resistance. If the pursuit of creativity as such proves easy to the point of triviality then there is the need for new difficulties, new restraints. I believe it would be possible to write the history of twentieth century art not in terms of revolutions and the overthrow of rules and traditions but rather as the continuity of a quest, a quest for problems worthy of the artist's nature. Whether we think of Picasso's restless search for creative novelty, or of Mondrian's impulse to paint, all the

Parallel Field
1990
Cast iron
187.5 × 45 × 35 cm

modernists may be described as knights errant in search of a challenge. Would
you accept this?

Havmann
1994-95
Granite
10.1 × 3.3 × 2.2 m
Mo-i-Rana, Norway

Gormley **I think it's true that this idea of a reaction against a kind of
orthodoxy is no longer a viable source of energy for art today. But I didn't
simply want to continue where Rodin left off, but re-invent the body from the
inside, from the point of view of existence. I had to start with my own
existence.**

Gombrich I think in your art also, you are trying to find some kind of restraint.
You want us to respond to the images of bodies, of your 'standard' body?

Gormley **I like that idea of a 'standard' body, but what I hope I've done is to
completely remove the problem of the subject. I have a subject, which is life,
within my own body. But in working with that I hope that it isn't just a
'standard' body: it is actually a particular one which becomes standardized
by the process ...**

Gombrich Because for you, your body is standard. It cannot be otherwise.

Gormley **What I'm doing is realizing, materializing perhaps for the first time,
the space within the body. It's certainly a very difficult thing to communicate,
but it's to do with meditation.**

Gombrich That has to do with breathing, with breath ...

Gormley **It has a lot to do with breath.**

Gombrich But you can't create what you breathe.

Gormley **No, but you can, I think, try to materialize the sensation of that inner
space of the body, and that's what I hope that these large body forms are.
They are in some way an attempt to realize embodiment, without really
worrying too much about mimesis, about representation in a traditional way.**

Gombrich About this internal body, this is something that must interest
anybody, but the question of whether it can be externalized is still another one,
isn't it? It starts from the most trivial fact that when we feel the cavities of our
own body, let us say the interior of the mouth, we have an entirely different
scale. Any crumb in our teeth feels very large and then when we get it out we are
surprised that it is so small, and if the dentist belabours your tooth you have the
feeling that the tooth is as large as you are. Then it turns out, if you look in the
mirror, that it was an ordinary small tooth. In a sense that is true of all internal
sensations: the internal world seems to have a different scale from the external
world.

Gormley **I think that's a brilliant, accessible example of what I'm interested in.
There was a repeated sensation that I had as a child before sleep, which was
that the space behind my eyes was incredibly tight, a tiny, dark matchbox,
suffocating in its claustrophobic imprisonment. And slowly the space would
expand and expand until it was enormous. In a way I feel that experience is**

Heavy Stones
1982
Stone
approx. 40 cm diam. each

still the basis of my work. This recent piece, *Havmann*, a 10-metre high black body mass, will read as a black hole in the sea, but it is made massively of stone. It's put at a distance from the viewer – 46 metres from the shore. Because there's an indeterminacy of scale in relation to the landscape, it is difficult to judge its actual size, which is an attempt to realize exactly the sort of thing you were saying.

Gombrich Of course, as you indicate, falling asleep, or even in dreams, this kind of sensation takes over. We are very much governed in our sleep by these body sensations which we project into some kind of outside world and see as things which they aren't. And you say that in Buddhist meditation this is also so, but it's not, because in Buddhist meditation you try to get away from thingness.

Gormley What I was trying to describe was the first experience of this inner body which was in my childhood. I think then the experience of learning Vipassana with Goenka in India was something very much more disciplined, but had to do with it. The minute you close your eyes in a conscious state you are aware of the darkness. With the Vipassana you explore that space in a very systematic manner. First of all you …

Gombrich You have to learn to relax.

Gormley **Well, it is an interesting mixture. Anapana, or mindfulness of breathing, gives you concentration. You then use that concentration to look at the sensation of being in the body, and that is a tool that I have tried to transfer to sculpture.**

Gombrich Yes, but my problem is how you bridge these very intense experiences which we can call 'subjective', a word which isn't very telling, and what you want the other to feel.

Gormley **That for me is the real challenge of sculpture. How do you make something out there, material, separate from you, an object amongst other objects, somehow carry the feeling of being – for the viewer to somehow make a connection with it. In a way, where you ended in *Art and Illusion* is where I want to begin. That idea that in some way there are things that cannot be articulated, that are unavailable for discourse, which can be conveyed in a material way, but can never be given a precise word equivalent for.**

Gombrich Certainly not. Our language isn't made like that. Our language serves a certain purpose, and that purpose is orientation of oneself and others in the three dimensional world. But I cannot describe the feeling I have in my thumb right now, the mixture between tension and relaxation. Sometimes if you go to the doctor you feel this helplessness in describing what your sensations are, there are no words. And that is a very important part of all human existence, that we have these limits. But your problem as far as I see it is to transcend these limits.

Gormley **I want to start where language ends.**

Gombrich But you want in a sense to make me feel what you feel.

Gormley **But I also want you to feel what you feel. I want the works to be reflexive. So it isn't simply an embodiment of a feeling I once had …**

Gombrich It's not the communication.

Gormley **I think it is a communication, but it is a meeting of two lives. It's a meeting of the expressiveness of me, the artist, and the expressiveness of you, the viewer. And for me the charge comes from that confrontation. It can be a confrontation between the movement of the viewer and the stillness of the object, which in some way is an irreconcilable difference, but also an invitation for the viewer to sense his own body through this moment of stillness.**

Gombrich In other words, what in early textbooks was called 'empathy', a

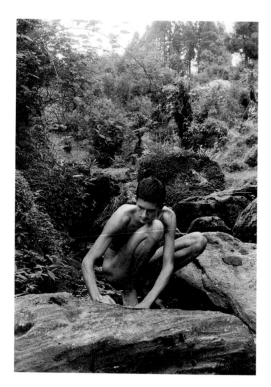

Antony Gormley in India
1973

Still Running
1986
Cast iron, air
168 × 66 × 102 cm
Collection, Umedalen Sculpture
Foundation, Umea, Sweden

feeling that you share in the character of a building, or a tree, or anything. I am always interested in our reaction to animals, because there we react very strongly. The hippopotamus has a very different character from the weasel, there is no doubt; we also talk to them in different ways. Our response is inevitable when dealing with the world around us.

Gormley **I think you are saying two things there. One is the anthropomorphizing of external stimuli and the other thing, which I am more interested in, is the idea of body size, mass; that a hippopotamus is huge and has rather a simple shape, and a weasel is like a line and sharp. It is also to do with speed; bodies themselves carry feeling which is in itself a kind of information that isn't available so easily to analysis. I want to use that empathy or embodiment in my work, and what I am trying to do is treat the whole body in the same way as perhaps portrait painters in the past have treated the face. I simply use my body as a starting point. I don't want to limit my sculptures autobiographically. On one level it is not dissimilar to choreography and the dancer's body. It is using the body as a medium.**

Gombrich It is not self-expression.

Gormley **I am interested in discovering principles. In a piece like** *Land, Sea and Air* **there is one standing body case,** *Sea,* **with the eyes open looking out to the horizon;** *Land* **is the crouching one which has ears and listens to the ground; and** *Air,* **the kneeling one, has its nose open. What I was trying to do there was find a bodily equivalent for an element through a perceptual gateway. I think that underlying my return to the human body is an idea of**

re-linking art with human survival. There isn't just a problem about what we can do next in art terms. In a sense this is where your field and my field mix. You have always been concerned with finding a value in art, the application of rational principles to the understanding of an emerging language, and I think that there has been a sense where art – certainly in the earlier part of the twentieth century – took a view of that history in order to validate its own vision. I think that it is more difficult to do that now. All of us are aware that Western history is one history amongst many histories, and in some way there now has to be a re-appraisal of where value has to come from. Subjective experience exists within a broader frame of reference. When you think about what happens next in art, it is very hard not to ask the question: what happens next in the development of global civilization?

Gombrich I agree with you in that the values of our civilization and the values of art are totally linked. One cannot have an art in a civilization which believes in no value whatever, therefore I quite agree with you in the central question. I think that all our response to art depends on the roots of our own culture, that is why it is quite hard to get to the root of Eastern art. I think that sometimes we can't understand the art of our own culture just as we don't understand the letters in Chinese calligraphy. Don't you agree?

Gormley **I think that it is invariably misunderstood, certainly at first experience, but my reply to the Chinese calligraphy question is my reply to anyone who finds it impossible to understand any one artist's work today. I think that if there is some sympathy there, then the invitation is to get more familiar. The idea that in some way value can only come from judging it from its own tradition, from which it may have escaped or never belonged to at all, is going to be less useful than looking at the organic development of an individual language and seeing if that has a universal significance. I would be interested to know whether you feel that it is possible to convey a notion of embodiment without mimesis, without having to describe, for instance, movement, or exact physiognomy.**

Gombrich I have no doubt that not only is it possible but it happens in our response to mountains, for example, we lend them our bodies. I think that the greater problem is the limit, because in a certain sense it happens all the time: it happens in the nursery, it happens in regressive states of the mind. The problem is not so much whether we can make people respond in this almost elemental form to shapes, but how to distinguish a work of art from a crumpled piece of paper, which also has its physiognomy and its character. I think there is partly still a feeling of a person behind it, which adds to the confidence of the viewer, that here is an embodiment and the viewer is interested in engaging in it.

Gormley **Yes I think that that idea of purpose is embodied in the way that something is put together, not just in its form. In some way that sense of purposefulness has to do with how clear the workmanship is, how ...**

Gombrich How manifest ...

Gormley **Yes.**

Land, Sea and Air II
1982
Lead, fibreglass
Land (crouching) 45 × 103 × 53 cm,
Sea (standing) 191 × 50 × 32 cm,
Air (kneeling) 118 × 69 × 52 cm

Gombrich It is really the 'mental set' in twentieth century art which is behind all these problems. You have to have a certain feel of what is going on there, otherwise it's just an object like any other.

foreground, **Heart**
1986
Lead
14.4 × 26.4 × 18 cm
background, **Room**
1986
Concrete
208 × 51 × 60 cm

Gormley **I think that we all are very visually informed these days. Maybe classical education within the visual arts has now been replaced by a multiplicity of visual images that come through computers and advertising and all sorts of sources.**

Gombrich Then you have the weirdest forms on TV, which I don't possess, and the sometimes amusing shapes created for advertising or whatever else. That is just the problem, the problem of the limits of triviality.

Gormley **Yes exactly. How do you condense from this multiplicity of images, certainly in sculpture, something that is still, silent, maybe rather complete, and therefore rather forbidding because it isn't like a moving image on a screen. It is not telling you to buy something. It's something that has a different relationship to life. And that for me is the challenge of sculpture now, that it may have within it a residue of 5,000 years of the body in art, but it must be approachable to somebody whose main experience of visual images is those things.**

Gombrich You want them to feel the difference between a superficial response of amusement and mild interest, and something that has a certain gravity.

Gormley **Yes, I think it should be a confrontation *(laughs)*.**

Gombrich Coming to terms with it.

Gormley **And through coming to terms with it, coming to terms with themselves.**

Gombrich Yes, perhaps that is a different matter.

Gormley **But that question of the difference between subjective response and the object is absolutely the essence of what I'm trying to get at. Whether this is something accessible to discourse is another matter. But for me, the idea that the space that the object embodies is in some way both mine and everyone's is very important, that it is as open to the subjective experience of the person looking at it as it is to me, the possessor of the body that gave that form in the first place.**

Gombrich You'll agree that everybody's experience is likely to be a little different.

Gormley **Absolutely. We have moved out of the age where you would argue that, yes that is a Madonna, but, well, the drapery isn't quite fully achieved. Today we have moved from signs that have an ascribed meaning and an iconography that we know how to judge, to a notion of signs that have become liberated. Now that has a certain annoyance factor *(laughs)*, but it also has a certain invitation for an involvement that was not possible before.**

Gombrich But it was with architecture.

Gormley **Yes that's true. And it's interesting that you mention architecture because I think of my work, certainly in its first phase, as being a kind of architecture. It's a kind of intimate architecture that is inviting an empathetic inhabitation of the imagination of the viewer.**

Gombrich But in architecture there was the constraint of the role of the tradition and purpose of a building. This is a church, and this is a railway station, and we approach them with slightly different expectations. The problem I think, which is not of your making, but is for every artist working today, is to establish some kind of framework wherein the response can develop.

Gormley **I'm working on it! I'd like us to talk a bit more about casting.**

Gombrich Well, did you know that it has turned out that part of Donatello's *Judith* is cast from the body? It's astonishing. I remember Rodin was charged with casting from the body, so it was considered a short cut, seen as very lazy or mean, or cheating.

Gormley **Absolutely, there's a prejudicial negative attitude.**

Gombrich Of course, quite a number of posthumous busts are based on the cast of the death mask that is usually modified. But this practice is not usually condemned.

Gormley **But it is interesting you see, because the in-built morbidity of the death mask is in some way in keeping with the idea of a memorial portrait…**

Gombrich It fits into what you call the context.

Gormley **But the interesting thing is that idea of trace. Certainly as a child, probably the most potent portraits which affected me in visits to the National Portrait Gallery were the portraits of Richard Burton, which was a rather dark oil painting, and the head of William Blake, which was a cast from life. What affected me as a child was feeling the presence of someone through the skin, where the contact of the skin with whatever was registering it, the impression, was not really as important as an idea somehow of a pressure behind the skin which was both physical and psychological.**

J. S. Deville
Life Mask of William Blake
c. 1807
Plaster
h. 27.6 cm

Gombrich It was alive in other words.

Gormley **No, it was more than that. There is a sense in which there is this pressure inside the dome of the scalp and then also this pressure behind the eyes which gives that work a kind of potency. It was as if something was trying to come through the surface of the skin. In a way the casting process in that instance, and I hope also in my work, is a way of getting beyond the minutiae of surface incident and instantly into that idea of presence, without there being something to do with interpretation. One of the bases of my work is that it has to come from real, individual experience. I can't be inside anyone else's body, so it's very important that I use my own. And each piece comes from a unique event in time. The process is simply the vehicle by which that event is captured, but it is very important to me that it's my body. The whole project is to make the work from the inside rather than to manipulate it from the outside and use the whole mind/body mechanism as an instrument, unselfconsciously, in so far as I'm not aware while I'm being cast of what it looks like. I get out of the mould, I re-assemble it and then I re-appraise the thing I have been, or the place that I have been and see how much potency it has. Sometimes it has none; I abandon it and start again.**

Gombrich What does the potency depend on?

Gormley **The potency depends on the internal pressure being registered.**

Gombrich And how much of this, in your view, is subjective and how much is inter-subjective?

Gormley **I am interested in something that one could call the collective** subjective. I really like the idea that if something is intensely felt by one individual that intensity can be felt even if the precise cause of the intensity is not recognized. I think that is to do with the equation that I am trying to make between an individual, highly personal experience and this very objective thing – a thing in the world, amongst other things. It is even constructed by objective principles; the plate divisions follow horizontal and vertical axes, but then they affect the viewer in a very subjective and particular way. I am not sure if I have any right to prescribe what the viewer should be thinking or feeling at that point. I would like to feel that there is a potential for his or her experience to be as intense as mine was, and equally subjective.

Gombrich You work as a guinea pig in a test to find out if it affects you. If the cast doesn't affect you, you discard it.

opposite, **Peer**
1984
Lead, plaster, fibreglass
188 × 50 × 43 cm

Gormley **Yes I think that has to be what I am judging when I see the immediate results of the body mould. What I am judging is its relationship to the feeling that I want the work to convey. Once I am out of it, it does become a more objective appraisal. I work very closely with my wife, the painter Vicken Parsons. Once we have defined what the position of the body will be then it is a matter of trying to hold that position with the maximum degree of concentration possible. Sometimes it's a practical thing; the position is so difficult to maintain that the mould goes limp. I lose it, I don't have the necessary muscular control and stamina to maintain it. More often and more interestingly it isn't those mechanical things but others that are more to do with intensity, and that can have to do with how much sleep I have had or simply with how in touch I am with what we are doing. The best work comes from a complete moment, which is a realization. I then continue to edit the work. It rarely involves cutting an arm off and replacing it with another but it may involve cutting through the neck and changing the angle two degrees. In terms of the process, we are talking about two stages, the first stage – and this is the most important because it is the foundation of the work – is making the mould. Then I go into the second stage which is making a journey from this very particularized moment to a more universal one, which is a process of adding skins. In the past this has meant I used different colours, to make sure that each layer was exactly the same thickness. Now I just rely on my judgement that I have reached the point at which this notion of a universal body and a particular body is in a state of meaningful equilibrium or meaningful balance.**

Work in progress
1986

Gombrich What you describe is a little like a painter stepping back from the canvas and judging it, examining it as if it were from the outside.

Gormley **It has to do with making the totality of the work count, as a whole, to deal with the mind/body as one organism, and re-present it as one organism rather than the current orthodoxy of the body in pieces, or the body as a battleground.**

Gombrich Now I will ask you a shocking question: why don't you take a photograph of your body?

Gormley **This is a photograph; I regard this as a three-dimensional photograph.**

Gombrich As you say a three-dimensional photograph, it could be done by holograph, there are methods. Would you accept it?

Gormley **No, that wouldn't interest me particularly. I am a classical sculptor in so far as I am interested in things like mass.**

Gombrich Tactility.

Gormley **Yes the tactility is very important and the idea of making a virtual**

reality for me denies the real challenge and the great joy of sculpture which is a kind of body in space.

Gombrich And of course it is to scale, while the photograph on the whole needn't be and can hardly be demonstrably to scale.

Gormley **The other problem with a photograph is that it is a picture, and I am not really interested in pictures, as I am not interested in illusion. This idea has in a way informed your book: the history of art as a succession of potential schema by which we are invited to make a picture of the world. As we evolve the visual language we continually revise the previous schema in order to find an illusion that works more and more effectively. I feel that I have left that whole issue behind in a sense, as one that has had its story. We have to find a new relationship between art and life. The task of art now is to strip us of illusion. To answer your question, how do we stop art from descending into formlessness/shapelessness? How do we find a challenge worthy of the artist's endeavour? My reply to that is, we have somehow to acknowledge the liberty of creativity in our own time which has to abandon tradition as a principle of validation, to abandon the tradition of mainstream Western art history and open itself up: any piece of work in the late twentieth century has to speak to the whole world.**

Gombrich It may have to, but it won't.

Editor What do you think of the question of your masculinity, vis à vis there being an idea about some universally recognizable experience?

Gormley **In some of the work, the sexuality is declared and relevant to the subject of the work and at other times it isn't. I have tried to escape from the male gaze, if we are thinking about the male gaze both in relation to nature as a place of slightly frightening otherness and the male gaze in relation to the female body as the object of desire, or the object of idealization. I think the idealization of my work and its relationship to landscape are very different from historical models. I am aware that the work is of a certain sex.**

Gombrich Well everybody belongs to a certain gender and a certain age, you can't get out of that and I think it's almost trivial isn't it, if you try to.

Gormley **Yes, but what I am saying is that I think that this is a modified maleness, without trying to be the orthodox new man, a lot of work tests the prescribed nature of maleness in various ways, but I can't deny the fact that it comes from a male body and from a male mind. Part of the reason that so much of the work tries to lay the verticality of the body down, or re-present it by putting it on the wall, is that I am aware that even when a body case is directly on the floor, because I am tall there is this sense of dominance, of a male confrontationality. So a work like *Close* attempts to relocate the body and relate it to the earth, takes what could have been a heroic stance and puts it into the position of vulnerability. *Close*, for me is an image of an adult body put in the position of a child. This could be conceived as being the traditional image of a mother and a child. The mother in this case being the earth, the child being the body that is clinging on.**

Close IV
1992
Iron
25 × 192 × 186cm
Courtyard of the Irish Museum of
Modern Art, Dublin

Gombrich You could also say it is a person prostrating himself, which is something different again, because then it is deliberate, humbling.

Gormley *Close* makes the body into a cross, completely fixes it. The body is almost used as a marker of a place, denying its own mobility in order to pick up on the idea that the earth is spinning at 1,000 km an hour around its own axis, and in order to talk about this illusion that we have of fixedness within the phenomenal world where in fact nothing is fixed. Close for me is a way of mediating the two forces, gravity and centrifuge; the body case becomes an instrument through which those forces are made palpable.

Editor You mentioned the cross and here is an angel, both historically symbolic forms. What meaning do they have for you?

A Case for an Angel II
1989
Plaster, fibreglass, lead,
steel, air
197 × 858 × 46 cm

Gormley I think that this is a question about religion and religious iconography. Religion tries to deal with big questions, and I hope that my art tries to deal with big questions like, 'who are we?', 'where are we going?'. The fact is that I grew up within a Christian tradition, those things are part of not only my intellectual make-up but images of self that were given to me as a child. But I don't see them as illustrations of those images, they are just part of the mental and emotional territory that I have to explore.

Editor They are not symbolic?

Gormley I don't want the work to be symbolic at all, I want the work to be as actual as it can be, which is why my version of an angel is a rather uncomfortable mixture between aeronautics and anatomy.

Gombrich Well the problem of how angels managed to fly with these relatively small wings is always present. But then their bodies probably have no weight; the wings are signs.

Gormley An interesting point, because it is this idea of a mediator between one level of existence and another...

Gombrich Of course, the *Angelos*, the messenger.

Post
1993
Cast iron
197 × 53 × 36 cm
Installation, Killerton Park, Exeter

Gormley **We need these means of transmission between one state of being and another. We cannot be bound by traditional meaning but at the same time it's important not to reject something simply because it has been done before, because in some senses we have to deal with everything. That is why I am as interested in placing my work in historical contexts, on the end of a pillar or in a church, as I am in the white cube of the gallery. I think that everything has to be accepted as part of the territory and that means accepting what has been necessary in the past for human beings, finding a way in which those needs can be expressed in a contemporary way that is not divisive or prescriptive in its interpretive function. I think that our attitude to history has changed, the idea of layering which also suggests a support structure has been replaced now by a co-existence of temporality. There is a sense in which my work exists within an understanding of historical precedent but also within a matrix of contemporaneity.**
I do want to ask you this one important question; I feel that you have done a lot for all of us in terms of making apparent the structures of our own visual culture and I get the feeling that you have a faith in the value of that story. I don't know what your faith is in the art of now, or of the future.

Gombrich About the future I know nothing. I am not a prophet. About the situation of the arts at present, I think that the framework of art at present is not a very desirable one, the framework of art-dealing, art shows and art criticism. But I don't think that it can be helped, it is part of destiny that art came into the situation and I think it has its own problems. Sensationalism and lack of concentration are not very desirable and not very healthy for art, but I don't despair of the future or at least the present of art. I wouldn't despair of the fact that there will always be artists as long as there are human beings who mind and who think this is an important activity.

Gormley **But do you feel that we are at the end of the story that you wrote?**

Gombrich No, of course not. I do feel that there is a disturbing element in the story, and in the new edition I am working on the intrusion of fashions in art, which has always existed. Romanticism has created an atmosphere that makes it harder for an artist to be an artist, because there are always seductive cries or traps which may tempt the artist, I wouldn't say art, to this kind of sensationalism, like exhibiting the carcass of a sheep – because they are talking points. The temptation to play at talking points becomes the pivot of what the young then want to do, also to have the same talking point. I think this is a social problem rather than a problem of art.

Gormley **It is very difficult not to start talking about such things without sounding sententious and moralistic, but I do feel that art is one of the last realms of human endeavour left that hasn't been tainted by ideologies that have proved constrictive. In some way art does have this potential to be a focus for life which can be removed from the constraints of moral imperative, but nevertheless can invite people to think about their own actions.**

Gombrich It has its own moral imperatives.

Gormley **It does for the artist making it. I think it is very, very difficult then to**

transfer that degree of moral commitment.

Gombrich It is not all that difficult. I mean the artist mustn't cheat. It's as simple as that.

Gormley **And he must take responsibility for his own actions.**

Gombrich And if he feels, as you just said, that something isn't good enough he must discard it. Self-criticism is part of this moral imperative, and has always been. It is the same whether you write a page or whatever you do; if it isn't good enough, you have to start again. It's as simple as that, isn't it? I once said it is a game which has only one rule, and the rule is that as long as you can think you can do better you must do it, even if it means starting again. Of course, from that point of view I don't think the situation has changed very much. I am sure that has always been the case.

Gormley **We keep touching on this problem of subjectivity and I don't think we are ever going to nail it down, but we have to replace the certainties of symbolism, mythology and classical illusion with something that is absolutely immediate and confronts the individual with his own life. Somehow truth has to be removed from a depicted absolute to a subjective experience, where value transfers from an external system that might be illustrated to one in which individual experience is held and given intensity.**

Gombrich I think your faith is a very noble one. I don't for a moment want to criticize it. The question with every faith is whether it holds in every circumstance, and that is a very different matter, isn't it?

Gormley **I think the idea of style as something that is inherited and with a kind of historical development now has to be replaced by an idea of an artist responsible to himself, to a language that may or not be conscious of historical precedent.**

Gombrich Quite, but there is a problem in your faith; would you expect from now on every artist to do what you do? Surely not.

Gormley **No, no.**

Gombrich Exactly, so it's only one form of solving the problem, isn't it?

Gormley **I think that we can no longer assume that simply because the right subject matter or the right means are being used that there is value in an artist's project. I think that the authority has shifted from an external validation to an internal one and I would regard that as the great joy of being an artist. The liberation of art today is to try to find, in a way, forms of expression that exist almost before language and to make them more apparent. I think that in an information age, in a sense, language is the one thing that we have plenty of, but what we need is a reinforcement of direct experience.**

Gombrich I fear this is a false trail; people always say if it could be said it

Fathers & Sons, Monuments & Toys, Gods & Artists
1985-86
Lead, plaster, fibreglass, air
Large figure, 245 × 57.6 × 48 cm
Small figure, 108 × 24 × 22 cm

wouldn't be painted and things of that kind. It is a triviality. Language serves a very different purpose. Language is an instrument, was created as an instrument. Cavemen said 'come here' or 'run, there are bison about', I mean it's quite clear that language is an instrument. Painting a bison is a very different thing from talking about a bison. Language is in statements, art is not. Language can lie. I would say that the majority of experiences are inaccessible to language, but it is astounding that some are.

Gormley I agree with your idea that in some way language is an orientation, but the point is that once you have oriented yourself, you then have to leap, you have to go somewhere. And then the question is whether you go into the known or into the unknown.

Contents

Learning to See III
1993
Lead, fibreglass, plaster, air
218 × 69 × 51 cm

I

To Meister Eckhart, art was religion and religion art. Artistic form, in his view, was a revelation of essence, a kind of revelation that is both living and active. 'Work', he wrote, 'comes from the outward and from the inner man, but the innermost man takes no part in it. In making a thing the very innermost self of a man comes into outwardness'[1]. The act of making, at its most creative, happens when the self and will are at rest; in that respect, therefore, it is impersonal.

Ananda Coomaraswamy, in his classic book, *Transformation of Nature in Art*, draws some significant parallels between Eckhart's thought and traditional Indian aesthetics. He explains that in India the formal element in art is considered to be a purely mental activity, and that the idea of 'pramāna', which implies the existence of 'types' or archetypes, is the basis of properly conceived design. 'Sādrśya', the correspondence of mental and sensational factors in a work of art, is at its heart.[2] What Eckhart, a medieval Christian mystic, and Indian aestheticians have in common is a belief that reality becomes perceptible when the intelligible and the sensible meet in the unity of being, one that is continuous and touches on the transcendent. This unity, like that achieved through yoga or certain mystical practices, is the realization of identity of consciousness with the object of love or attention.

Much of Antony Gormley's art is based on his understanding of Western and Eastern spiritual traditions, and his work resonates when it is placed in this context. Like Eckhart – or, indeed, like Joseph Beuys – Gormley believes that the artist is not a special kind of man, but that every man is a special kind of artist. He would have some sympathy with Eckhart's notion that it as an 'artist-scholar' that man prepares all things to return to God, in so far as he sees them intellectually and not merely sensibly. He works with 'types', with universals, and yet he roots his work in subjective experience. Besides, like classical Indian works of art, Gormley's sculptures have an identifiable 'rasa', or 'essence', with which the viewer must identify, and which can lead to a sense of infinite timelessness. But what concerns Gormley, more than anything else, is the paradoxical manner in which man, while containing infinite space, is also contained by it.

Gormley's project, despite its metaphysical underpinnings, is far from otherworldly. His sculpture deals with what he sees as the 'deep space' of the interior of the body, yet he is also concerned with 'touch as gravity' and 'gravity as the attraction that binds us to the earth'. Its key strength, perhaps, lies in the artist's determination to accept nothing until it has been lived and internalized. Gormley's work is structured and methodical, preconceived to a certain point, and then realized in the process of making.

If it can be said that Gormley's lead body cases create tension between the perception of a body within space and that of a space within the body, then a piece such as *Learning to See* tends towards the latter side of the correspondence. As he has explained, with reference to its genesis, 'I have acknowledged the eyes, which I normally avoid. They are closed but suggest that I am becoming conscious of the space within the body'.[3]

Yet what Gormley has referred to as a 'dynamic' between the body as 'a thing' and as 'a space' could just as readily be seen as an unresolved conflict. In many interviews and writings he has alluded to his belief that the physical body is inseparable from consciousness; sometimes he describes it as a kind of prison, with its various orifices the only conduits between the inner self and the outside world, and occasionally as a 'temple' of being. But although this vacillation between the reluctant acceptance of the body as a temporary home for the spirit and its enthusiastic celebration as one of the wonders of creation may be characteristic of the Catholic ethos in which Gormley was raised, it is not the only – and perhaps not even the main – source of that conflict.

The phrase 'Learning to See', as the title of a piece of figurative sculpture with closed eyes, suggests that the vision in question is inward, not outward. The work's leaden skin, which both seals and protects, allows for no interaction between outer and inner space; it is an impermeable membrane. Significantly, too, the artist has chosen to describe the sculpture as being made from 'air', as well as from lead and fibreglass, as if to stress that what we can't perceive with our eyes is very much an aspect of its construction. 'Seeing', in this context, might therefore be defined as 'insight'.

The word 'insight', coincidentally, is often used as the translation of 'vipassana', a Pali term which, in conjunction with 'bhāvanā', is the name given to the Buddhist meditation practice that Gormley studied for two years in India. This meditational method, based on awareness and attention, eschews metaphysical speculation

and encourages the development of 'sati', or 'mindfulness', a kind of unselfconscious awareness of the present moment. Vipassana meditation brings attention to bear on the ways in which ideas and sensations arise and disappear; thus, it is claimed, detachment and freedom are generated. This, in part, is because all Buddhist teachings are posited on the acceptance of 'impermanence' and 'non-self' as laws of life: all things, sensations and thoughts are conditioned, relative, and interdependent. 'Desire', or 'craving', is the energy that keeps the circle of becoming in motion; right 'mindfulness' is one of the ways in which desire can be dissipated and the chain of 'causation' broken.

Gormley has spoken of the influence of Vipassana training on the making of his sculpture, especially in its stress on the development of 'awareness' of the body. The Buddhist idea of 'impermanence', however, is not quite so dominant in his thinking. Gormley's lead sculptures are not unambiguous in their effect on the viewer. Conveying an impression of weight and solidity, his sculptures seem as much the precise registrations of a fixed sense of self as impressions of a constantly mutable body. Nonetheless, as can be seen in the generic, anonymous form of the cases, Gormley also appears to be drawn towards a more impersonal conception of identity. It is here – not so much in a conflict between Christianity and Buddhism, but in the relation between 'I' and 'not-I' – that the energy of his work is born.

To Gormley, the body has a relation to the external space within which it exists as well as to the inner space it contains. And in an installation made for

Old Jail, Charleston, exterior

'Places with a Past', a 1991 exhibition of site-specific art at Charleston, South Carolina, Gormley combined a series of works – *Host, Field, Three Bodies, Learning to Think, Fruit* and *Cord* – in order to explore that relationship. The Old City Jail, which contained and became part of the installation, could be described as having the shape of a body: the original rectangular structure is rather like a torso; its later octagonal addition, like a head. And in order to emphasize its parallels with his body cases, which are sometimes connected to the outside world through orifices, Gormley removed the boards and glazing that had sealed up the prison's doors and windows. This allowed light and sound to enter the prison, to enliven what had hitherto been dark and dormant, and to engage time as an active element in the installation. In the artist's words, 'the building became a catalyst for reflection on liberty and incarceration'[4].

The prison's physical structure, because its floor plan allows for the pairing of spaces, offered Gormley a rare opportunity to develop the dialectical oppositions and correspondences that are central to his project. On the second floor, *Field*, a set of terracotta figurines, faced a similar vast space that contained only *Three Bodies* – large metal spheres, made of steel and air, which the artist has described as 'like celestial bodies fallen from the sky'[5]. Above *Field* was *Learning to Think*, five headless lead body cases that were suspended from the ceiling, in a contradictory evocation of both lynching and ascension. The corresponding space held *Host*, a room containing mud and sea-water – 'The surface of the earth described in Genesis ... the unformed, the place of possibility, a

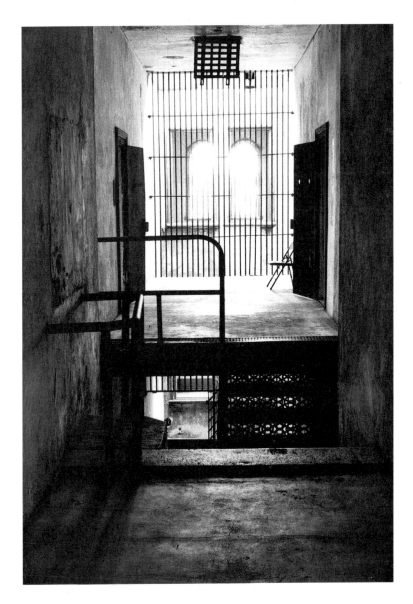

Old Jail, Charleston, interior

overleaf
top left, **Host**
1991
Mud, seawater
Depth, 13 cm

bottom left, **Field**
1991
Terracotta, approx. 35,000 figures
Variable size, 8-26 cm each

right, **Three Bodies**
1991
Steel, air
3 spheres, diam. 123 cm each

Learning to Think
1991
Lead, fibreglass, air
5 body cases, 173 × 106 × 31 cm
each

place waiting for the seed', according to Gormley[6].

In the octagonal extension, two related organic forms, *Fruit*, were hung on either side of a wall. Only one was visible at a time, in order 'to reconcile opposites not in terms of differentiation but by mirroring'[7]. Hidden from view, and at the centre of each sculpture, was a space once occupied by the artist's own body, linked to the other side, through mouth and genitals, by steel pipes. The final piece was *Cord*, made of many tubes inside one another – a kind of umbilical lifeline between the 'seen' and 'unseen'.

In this installation, one of great richness and complexity, Gormley brought into play the full panoply of his ambition. Working with lead and clay, as well as with the four elements, Gormley alluded to physical and spiritual containment, body and mind, outer and inner worlds, feeling and thinking, birth and death, growth and decay. And if the contradictions inherent in *Learning to See* give strength to the artist's conception of inner vision, the dualities evoked by the installation at Charleston are subservient to a sense of passage towards expansiveness. The emotional depth of the work can be ascribed to its refusal to exclude either the particular or the universal: it encompasses both historical specificity and a sense of shared human experience. In formal terms, this is achieved by the undermining of the Modernist notion of the self-referential object. While each of the elements of the installation can be separately contemplated, they are most meaningful when perceived as parts of a larger whole. In that sense, they are like parts of a body.

opposite, top and bottom, **Fruit,**
Parts One and Two
1991
Plaster, mica, oyster shell, jute,
wood, steel
370 × 215 × 120 cm

above, **Cord**
1991
Copper, plaster
340 × 0.4 cm

II

Maurice Merleau-Ponty, whose philosophy of phenomenology deeply influenced much art of the 1970s, has written about the 'dialectical imagination' that is marked by a Hegelian drive towards synthesis and synergy. Imagination, he believed, can have privileged access to the hidden dimensions of Being – to what, in his later writings, he calls 'the invisible'. This, he said, can be imagined but not seen; it is not non-existent but pre-exists in the visible. Every 'visible' dimension of being, for Merleau-Ponty, is correlatively connected to an invisible or imaginary dimension; he sought to establish the real and the imaginary as two separate but corresponding realms: separate on the level of ordinary being but corresponding on the level of fundamental Being. Such correspondence applied even to the human body – 'It is not the utilizable, functional, prosaic body which explains man: on the contrary, the body is precisely human to the extent that it discovers its symbolic and poetic charge'[8].

Gormley, like Merleau-Ponty, is much drawn to the idea of correspondence between the visible and invisible; he has also said that his interest in the body was aroused because embodiment, or being-in-the-world, provided him with a way of escaping from the dualism of dialectics. In other words, to Gormley the body is the articulation of meaning; it is that in which sense is given and out of which sense emerges[9].

Jacob Epstein
Elemental
1932
Alabaster
h. 81 cm

William Blake
Jerusalem, Vala, Hyle and Skofeld
1804-5/1820
Line engraving printed in relief,
watercolour
15.5 × 22.2 cm

As Gormley understands it, the representation of the body in Western art, at least since the Renaissance, has been centred on the expressiveness of movement: the relationship between mind and body, or spirit and matter, has conventionally been expressed through the tension of man struggling against the forces of nature[10]. This expression, until the onset of Modernism, has always been mimetic. With abstraction, however, came the apparent end of the figurative tradition. Yet, as Stephen Bann has noted, the dominance of abstraction simply marked the end of mimesis, of the 'essential copy' of the figure. And Gormley, according to Bann, has set himself the task of extricating himself from Modernism without breaking the mould.

What Gormley has conspicuously retained from Modernist practice is its utopianism – he believes that art has the power to change things for the good. And being part of the generation that grew up with Minimalism, his thought, as already noted, has certain parallels in the phenomenology that was influential in the 1960s and 1970s. But what is also clear is the way Gormley reads Minimalism not as a rupture in Modernist sculptural tradition but as a reinforcement of its continuities.

As he has acknowledged, Gormley's encounter with Jacob Epstein's sculpture, *Elemental*, in 1981, was a crucial moment in that task of reintegration. This is interesting for two reasons. Firstly, it aligns Gormley with a non-conformist, figurative, strand in British art – one that extends from William Blake, through Eric Gill, to Stanley Spencer. (All of these are artists with whom he has a pronounced sympathy.) Secondly, *Elemental* has a certain primeval, or 'primitive'

quality: it recalls Jean-Luc Nancy's observation that 'the body was born in Plato's cave, or rather it was conceived and shaped in the form of the cave: as a prison or tomb of the soul, and the body first was thought from the inside, as buried darkness into which light only penetrates in the form of reflections, and reality in the form of shadows'[11]. *Elemental* suggests heaviness, slow awakening, and enclosure. It is about beginnings.

While Epstein, in the 1940s, found himself somewhat isolated in his rejection of the Modernist abstraction of Barbara Hepworth and Henry Moore, his determination to restore more 'human' values to British art was not unique. For the best part of two decades after World War II, figurative and humanist work was dominant in the visual arts; only after 1960 did leading sculptors, like Anthony Caro, revive interest in abstract, constructed sculpture. Nonetheless, when Gormley decided, after seeing *Elemental*, to make sculptures that more vividly reflected his own feelings, his shift in direction was unusual: new British sculpture in the early years of the decade was predominantly remarkable for its 'urban' sensibility. Tony Cragg and Bill Woodrow worked with the detritus of contemporary life; Richard Deacon and Alison Wilding had more formalist interests. Gormley's concerns, however, like those of Anish Kapoor, were described at the time as being centred on 'the mystery and wonder of creation, the cycle of life itself and the dichotomy between the physical and the intellectual ... '[12]

Lynne Cooke, writing about Gormley's work during that period[13], perceptively recognized its idiosyncrasies. Gormley, she observed, chose to

top to bottom

Bill Woodrow
Twin Tub with Guitar
1981
Washing machine
76 × 89 × 66 cm

Tony Cragg
Paddle
1984
Plastic angle pipe and wooden
paddle
34 × 153 × 42 cm

Alison Wilding
All Night Through
1986
Leaded steel, brass, rubber
103 × 500 × 113 cm

Anish Kapoor
1000 Names (Nos. 22 to 26)
1981
Wood, gesso, pigment
Five objects,
122 × 183 × 183 cm overall

represent 'rudimentary' and 'elementary' experiences, which were neither primitive nor archetypal. Nor were his figures recognizable individuals: 'his casts are not like George Segal's, whose emphasis on modern dress and contemporary contexts they do not share, nor are they in the expressive tradition of Rodin, whose broken surfaces present the body as a "mirror of the soul"'. His body cases were not 'surrogate human beings'; rather, she noted, Gormley's body casts are 'containers', a difference that is emphasized by the joins and welds on their surfaces. His works being less than comfortable in a Modernist context, she suggested that it might be more appropriate to relate them to Indian sculpture and iconic Western art. Gormley's images, Cooke proposed, should be contemplated, not interpreted, and – crucially – brought to life by the viewer's engagement with them.

This kinship with the ideals of Indian sculpture is not, of course, surprising; Gormley has spoken of his admiration for 6th century Jain sculpture and Southern Indian bronzes[14], remarking that he was much impressed by their 'stillness' (a quality that is possessed by the majority of his own body cases). In the same interview, Gormley also drew attention to the twin forces of will and containment that 'create' the feeling of stillness. He explained that, in order to hold a position long enough for the artist, Vicken Parsons, to cover him with clingfilm, followed by scrim and plaster, he makes a concentrated act of attention; then, gradually, the drying plaster becomes substantial and starts to hold him in place. The process, therefore, is a kind of mummification or entombment which, in time,

is followed by release.

Interestingly, Stephen Bann has noted, referring to Jacob Epstein's work of the same name, that 'Lazarus is indeed a precedent to bear in mind when looking at Gormley's sculpture, since the image of the decayed body brought suddenly back to life conflicts so decisively with the ideal, heroic tradition of sculpture which we derive from the Greeks'[15]. Gormley's project, he argues, is central to the revitalization of the figurative tradition, largely because of the 'dynamic relationship which (he) establishes between the work and its spatial context'. Concurrently, Gormley's concern is 'with moving beyond the barrier of appearance, and posing questions about our place in the created world'.

Elsewhere[16], Bann expands this line of thinking. With a work like *Lost Subject*, the viewer is able, he suggests, to establish a direct, unmediated relationship with Gormley's sculpture because it transgresses the line between reality and representation: the figures are 'body cases', cast from the artist himself. This is also a semiotic issue: the figure is an indexical sign, not a symbol. As an example of a comparable sign, Bann mentions the plaster moulds taken from the bodies left in the earth of Pompeii after the eruption of Vesuvius. And although the title of the piece is partly a reference to the traditional *circe perdu* technique of casting, its main purpose is to alert the viewer to the importance of filling the 'loss' himself. It also reminds us that *Lost Subject* does not show an ideal body, in the classical tradition, nor is it expressively modernist. Instead, 'it is precisely a body conceived as the mediation between

below, **St. Allard's Foot**
1331
Reliquary

bottom, **Rise**
1983–84
Lead, fibreglass, plaster, air
30 × 58 × 190 cm

interiority and exteriority – working through the indexical effect of surface'.

The crux of Gormley's sculptural strategy, according to Bann, is the evocation of 'presence'. As a comparison, he refers to a medieval reliquary which represents the foot of St. Allard. This reliquary, he argues, is both a mould and a container: 'It contains relics of the saint's foot; therefore the inside is crucial, even if we cannot see what is there. It also takes the outward form of a foot – not, however, the foot as perishable flesh and bone, but as part of the glorified body of the martyr'. Quoting the view of German philosopher Hans Georg Gadamer, that religious art – characterized by a deliberate confusion or contagion between the object and referent – is the

type of all art, Bann suggests that the traditional idea of representation is not a norm universally applicable to the arts. Gormley's wish to make sculpture that is 'a vehicle for feeling', he goes on, reflects his rejection of that convention and his proximity to a tradition of imagemaking 'where the prime consideration is not that a sculpture should stand for or represent the body and its parts, but actually indicate the presence of the body'.

In conclusion, Bann proposes that Gormley's work should not be read in modernist or formalist terms, but that it impels us to search for comparisons outside conventional areas of discussion. This also means, he notes, that his sculptures 'require us to look beyond the objects themselves to the systems of belief which underlie representation'.

Lost Subject I
1994
Lead, fibreglass, air
25 × 145 × 228 cm
Collection, Israel Museum,
Jerusalem

top, **Caspar David Friedrich**
The Monk and Sea
1808-09
Oil on canvas
110 × 171.5 cm

above, **Edvard Munch**
Melancholy
1894
Oil on canvas
81 × 100.5 cm

left, **A View: A Place**
1985-86
Lead, plaster, fibreglass
197 × 57 × 40 cm

III

Antony Gormley's sculptural project reveals an obsession with grand, emotive issues, such as birth, death, and man alone with his fate. In his works on paper, moreover, the artist's intense subjectivism becomes apparent: the body is not so much seen from the outside as felt from the inside; expressive of the physical and spiritual experience of being embodied on earth, they are about fear as well as joy. A typical figure in one of Gormley's drawings, as Michael Newman has written, 'is not standardized and ideal, but can be small or large; it is not isolated and complete in itself but interacts with the space and light and dark areas around itself. The world is a container for the body which in turn is a vessel … The body can be opened up, the inside extruded into the outside, or it can be joined with another body in sexual activity. The process of making the drawing is an analogy to the state of becoming and change in which we all live'[17].

A recurring image in Gormley's works on paper is a solitary person, turned away from the viewer and facing open natural expanses of water or sky. Were their mood one of harmony and self-loss, these drawings would be reminiscent of the sublimity of Caspar David Friedrich, but because their aura tends to be dark and anguished, they are more likely to recall the work of Edvard Munch. In contrast to his sculptures, which – at least in part – act as neutral receptacles for the viewer's own feelings and projections, the inner space of Gormley's drawings attest to the vulnerability of openness. They are predominantly melancholic.

Untitled
1985
Oil and charcoal on paper
25.5 × 34 cm

Home and the World
1985
Oil and charcoal on paper
25.5 × 34 cm

Land, Sea and Air II

above left, **Air**
1982
Lead, fibreglass
118 × 69 × 52 cm

above right, **Sea**
1982
Lead, fibreglass
191 × 50 × 32 cm

left, **Land**
1982
Lead, fibreglass
45 × 103 × 53 cm

Gormley believes that this melancholia is symptomatic of the general malaise of contemporary Western society which also shows signs of fin-de-siècle disillusion and, albeit to a lesser extent, of pessimistic millenarianism. Shearer West, in her study of these phenomena[18], suggests that their characteristic is a heightened awareness of the passing of time and the sense that history is moving towards a final conclusion. These transitional periods, she proposes, seem to heighten general consciousness of disruptions, disasters, and catastrophes, with a consequent rise in millennium prophesies, utopian visions, and other 'spiritual' occurrences. Thus, at the end of the nineteenth century, following massive growth of European cities and the development of industrial technology, writers and artists of the 'aesthetic' movement rejected the dominant positivist ideology of the day, turning their attention to subjective, symbolic, and otherwise 'decadent' thoughts. A paradigm of the 'fin-de-siècle' mentality, according to Shearer, is Schopenhauer's notion, developed in *The World as Will and Idea*, that mankind is a mass of individuals whose wills are permanently in conflict, and whose only reliable solace is in a contemplative form of religious experience. This is a view with which Gormley would appear to concur.

One of the seminal pieces in the development of Gormley's sculpture is *Land, Sea and Air II*, in which the process of Buddhist 'awareness' is embodied by human figures in three elemental postures: they stand, kneel and crouch. In their original setting – on the seashore – one figure has his ear to the ground, another kneels with his head raised, as if in awe or supplication, while the third stares out to sea. This configuration (in the artist's view, three is the 'beginning of infinity') evokes completeness and harmony: a sense of atonement with the self and with the world.

Because they are conceived in a positive spirit of stillness and awareness, it is significant that Gormley's body-cases are normally made of lead, a substance that is traditionally associated with Saturnine melancholy. Gormley has given varied reasons for his use of the material; lead, he explains, is ordinary, malleable, dense, undecaying, and permanent. It also has a mercurial property that allows for the creation of surfaces that subtly reflect light while absorbing it, a quality he is careful to maintain by not allowing it to oxidize. Important, too, are its protective qualities: lead is a shield; it is impenetrable visually and radioactively. (In earlier works, such as *Natural Selection*, in which natural and artificial objects were encased in lead, their insulation from radioactive fallout was central to the artist's intention. See pages 126-27.) But lead is also heavy, poisonous, and chemically irreducible – qualities that are of relevance in its role in alchemical practice. Another association (which is also crucial in Anselm Kiefer's use of the same material) is its identification, in alchemy and the Jewish kabbala, with primordial matter.

Anselm Kiefer
Outpour
1982-86
Mixed media on canvas

Word Made Flesh
1989
Iron, air
65 × 62 × 53 cm
Collection, Museum of
Contemporary Art, Los Angeles

Untitled
1981
Charcoal and oil on paper
60 × 84 cm

While, from some perspectives, the lead body cases appear buoyant and optimistic, they can also be perceived as isolation chambers. They then become suggestive of retreat, either to the tomb or the womb, and seem to be founded on a wish to preserve, untouched, a fragile state of being. As James Hall has pointed out, Gormley's living death wish reminds one of Freud's comments about living burial in his 'Essay on the Uncanny'. For some people, Freud wrote, the idea of ' being buried alive by mistake is the most uncanny thing of all', and yet this 'terrifying fantasy' is only a transformation of another fantasy which has originally nothing terrifying about it at all – the fantasy of intra-uterine existence[19].

The notion of 'entombment', however, is not as negative as it may, at first, appear. In Christian belief resurrection follows death and, in a closer parallel to this reading of Gormley's body cases, alchemical thought describes the regression into the darkness of 'nigredo' as the necessary prelude to rebirth: in a sealed vessel the transformation of the 'prima materia' takes place. (Some commentators[20], interpreting alchemical ideas from a psychological perspective, have suggested that the alchemical sealed vessel is comparable to the state of introversion that acts as a container for the transmutation of attitudes and emotions.)

It is worth noting, too, that *Passage* and *Word Made Flesh*, which are among the more unusual of Gormley's body cases, echo ancient resurrection imagery. In the Egyptian tomb of Sethi the First, there is a drawing of a house guarded by two sphinxes in which the rebirth of the sun god takes place. The sun god is represented as an icthyphallic man lying on his back with an erect phallus. Around him is an Ouroboros, the snake that swallows its own tail. And another comparable work, *Matter*, in which a bulbous clay phallus appears to be growing of its own accord on top of a reclining figure, recalls an old alchemical drawing of the fallen Adam, resting on the ground with a living tree rooted in his loins[21].

above, **Adam as *prima materia*, pierced by the arrow of Mercurius**
14th c.

left, **Matter**
1985
Lead, plaster, fibreglass, clay, air
54 × 56 × 208 cm

Body
1990
Bronze, air
202 × 84 × 65 cm
Installed Casino Monte Carlo,
Monaco

Fruits of the Earth
1978-79
Lead, revolver, bottle of wine,
machette
Largest element, approx. 60 cm

IV

There is a shamanic aspect to the ritual of self-entombment that is the first step in the making of Gormley's body cases. Mary Douglas has pointed out that such 'rehearsals' of death, in tribal contexts, are expected to engender beneficial changes in external events. But as the shaman knows well, while punishments, moral pressures and a ritual framework can do something to bring man into harmony with the rest of being, fulfilment is imperfect so long as free consent is withheld. As Douglas describes it, 'escape from the chain of necessity lies only in the exercise of choice'. And 'when someone embraces freely the symbols of death, or death itself, then ... a great release of power for good should be expected to follow'[22].

The willing embrace of death, of course, is a heroic undertaking, one that is not easily fulfilled. And although works like *Field* and *Lost Subject* reflect the significance Gormley places on self-abandonment, the latter's companion piece demonstrates the ego's reluctance to yield its position of primacy. According to the artist[23], *Close* illustrates a point of equilibrium between centrifuge and gravity; it represents the idea of a return to the body, and through the body a return

to the earth. But as Gormley also acknowledges, the piece is full of contradictions. Does the body cling to the earth out of choice or necessity? Is the pose indicative of humble self-abasement or a desperate desire to cling on to the world ? Or, put otherwise, can the lead case be interpreted as a symbol of resistance to the Christian doctrine of glorification of the body in its materiality? Is Gormley's project nearer to the mythologies of the Greeks and the Romans, in which the body is involved in a process of metamorphosis, as opposed to self-transcendence[24]?

This possibility is suggested by several of the early lead pieces, such as *Fruits of the Earth*, which contain objects that, having been encased in layer upon layer of lead, turn into ovoid shapes; similarly, some of the later cases, like *Body*, expand to the point where they begin to lose definition. (They are subsequently transmuted into the large 'expansion' pieces that have barely any resemblance to the figures they 'contain'.) What these disparate works all reflect is the intimation that while there may be some kind of rebirth after the destruction of the self, this may not take the form of a recognisable 'resurrected' body.

ANTONY GORMLEY

'VEHICLE'

Vehicle
1987
Lead, fibreglass, wood, steel, air
147 × 750 × 1520 cm
Installation, Salvatore Ala Gallery,
New York

When Gormley speaks about his work as an 'attempt to materialize uncertainty' and 'to isolate some point of contact between consciousness and matter', and when he alludes to 'the dispersion of self through awareness'[25], he is closer to Buddhist thinking than to Christian faith. It has been suggested that a group of works of the late 1980s – a quartet of pairs of lead boxes surmounted by internal organs made of stone – refer to Indian theories about 'chakras', or energy centres[26], but while this may be so, yogic practice is not central to Gormley's project. What is vital, though, is the sense of composure and self-awareness that Buddhism teaches, for this is frequently manifested in Gormley's work. In *A Case for an Angel*, for instance, there is a fine balance between a feeling of reverence at the splendour of mankind's aspirations towards the infinite and the calm acceptance that, as human beings, we are necessarily grounded on the earth. Like *Vehicle*, *A Case for an Angel* is an image of the body as a continuum between spirit and matter; it has been described by the artist as ' a being that might be more at home in the air, brought down to earth … It is also an image of somebody who is fatally handicapped, who cannot pass through any door and is desperately burdened'[27].

overleaf
Installation, Louisiana Museum,
Humlebaek, Denmark, 1989
l. to r., **Earth Above Ground**, 1986-
87; **Landing**, 1988-89; **Meaning;
Body and Light**, 1988/93; **12
Hours: the Beginning, the
Middle, the End**, 1983-84;
Present Time, 1987-88; **Fold**,
1988

Offering
1992
Iron, air
195 × 64 × 40 cm

In keeping with both Christian and Buddhist spiritual traditions, Gormley moves to the point where the familiar sense of self has to be abandoned; in a piece like *Field*, that threshold is intrinsic to the work. But the self is adamant; it does not readily lie down to die. Some of Gormley's more beautiful pieces are those, like *Rise, Earth Above Ground* and *Offering*, which most incisively objectify the self's will-to-live. In works like these, as in the recent *Testing a World View*, the overarching humanism of Gormley's project becomes apparent. We are embodied; we are conscious. Everything else is uncertain.

This struggle to come to terms with anxiety and uncertainty gives sinew to Gormley's project, as well as being the cause of unexpected moments of humour: as on a Möbius strip, to travel far enough along one approach to Gormley's work is to find oneself on its opposite. Thus *Word Made Flesh* and *Passage*, their similarities with alchemical imagery notwithstanding, are oddly transgressive; *Peer* and *Tree* have a wonderful sense of absurdity; *Address* is splendidly irreverent. Seen in this light, even the fruitlike 'expansion' pieces can appear scatological. From this aspect, Keith Haring, Charles Ray and Robert Gober can be seen to be Gormley's companions along the way; similarly, it becomes apparent that holiness and unholiness need not always be absolute opposites, for as Mary Douglas has observed, 'pollution symbols are as necessary as the use of black in any depiction whatsoever. Therefore we find corruption enshrined in sacred places and times'[28].

opposite

Tree

1984

Lead, fibreglass, plaster, air

472 × 60 × 30 cm

right

Still Falling

1990

Iron, air

334 × 115 × 85 cm

Collection, Irish Museum of

Modern Art, Dublin

V

In an early presentation, Antony Gormley spoke about the fundamental premises on which he based his project[29]. His work, he said, called upon the active participation of the viewer; it tried to allow things and materials that already exist to become eloquent rather than generating expressive forms in their own right; and it was a re-presentation of structures in the world. At the end of the talk, in which he described the development of his sculpture upto and including the first lead pieces, such as *Natural Selection*, Gormley mentioned that his approach combined the intellectual and the physical, and that it was predominantly about 'cutting open' and 'making vulnerable'. Sacrifice, he said, seems to be necessary for things to be reborn and seen anew.

One of the more interesting aspects of Gormley's early work is the constant dialectic between the organic materials he employed and his formal strategies, influenced by Arte Povera and Minimalism. Some early works, like *Sleeping Places* and *Bed*, have formal links with Robert Morris, Carl Andre and Mario Merz, just as other pieces, such as *Breadline*, recall Richard Long. *Rearranged Tree*, for example, in which the artist cut up the trunk of a thirty-foot pine and set out the slices in a spiral, is an attempt to suggest a sense of time using the idiom of space. *Bed*, a piece that is both elegiac and humourous, contains two impressions of the artist's body – the spaces having been eaten out of an ordered 'mattress' of processed bread.

top right
Mario Merz
Alligator
1989
Glass, steel, neon numbers
Installed, MoCA, Los Angeles

above
Carl Andre
Equivalent VIII
1966
Plaster
229 × 12.7 × 68.6 cm

right
Richard Long
Clearing a Path, A Six Day Walk in the Hoggar, the Sahara
1988
Photography and text
79.2 × 108 cm

above, far left
Mothers Pride
1982
Bread, wax
305 × 190 × 0.8 cm

above
Bread Line
1981
Bread
1 × 1500 × 3 cm
Installation, 'Objects and
Sculptures', ICA, London,
also showing works by Richard
Deacon, Anish Kapoor and
Peter Randall Page

left
Flat Tree
1978
Larch wood
6.78 m diam.

overleaf
Bed
1981
Bread, wax
28 × 220 × 168 cm

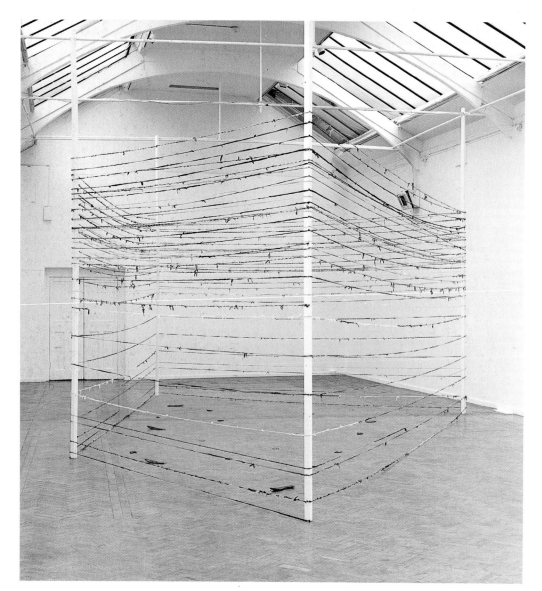

Room
1980
Socks, shoes, pants, trousers,
shirt, pullover, vest, jacket, wood

this period, 'the mystery is with the skin ... In Gormley's aesthetic, nothing lies 'inside' anything. *Full Bowl* is a bowl where the inside is described by the same means as the outside; there is no final edge ... The skin on a body or the meniscus on water are physical manifestations of Antony Gormley's actual mystery: the edge between definitions; the place where surface begins or ends ...[30]'

He also identifies an interest that was shared by many contemporary British sculptors. 'After more than two decades the biomorphic form has again become a central concern within British sculpture', Stuart Morgan wrote. 'In the early fifties this concern was characterized by an interest in structure, in the skeleton as the framework of the body. Today ... we find a comparable fascination with surface, with the skin as an envelope of the form. The skin is the visible appearance, the surface which establishes the boundary, the defining edge, the volume within and the space without ... In all (this) work is an underlying but pervasive sense of flux, of objects changing in form, shape or appearance. The skin becomes the visible manifestation of this process ...[31]'

This point is clearly realized in the *Sleeping Places*, which are among the most beautiful of Gormley's early works. Inspired by seeing people sleeping on the platforms of railway stations in India, these pieces, made from sheets covering recumbent bodies and immersed in plaster, convey a strong sensation of inner space – and, like *Bed*, of the ambiguous line between absence and presence. The *Sleeping Places* were nothing but skins, the fragile containers of private space.

But perhaps more enduring, at least in terms of the subsequent development of his work, were his observations about skin, which he described as a container of 'personal space'. This idea informed *Room*, a continuous strip of cut-up clothing which enclosed a twenty-foot square, and *Exercise between Blood and Earth*, which was a 'diagram of the active influence surrounding a man'. Starting with an image of a running figure, Gormley expanded the drawing's contours until they conformed to an almost perfect circle described by the radius of his arm. And as Stuart Morgan remarked, writing about another work of

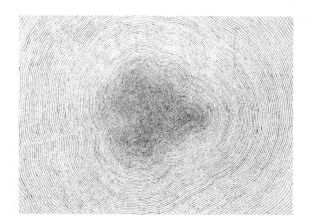

Exercise between Blood and Earth
1979-1981
Chalk on wall
184 cm diam.

below
Full Bowl
1977-78
Lead
6 × 17 × 17 cm

right
Full Bowl (dismantled)
1977-78
Lead

left
My Clothes
1980
The artist's clothes: shirt, jumper, vest, pants, socks, trousers

below
Sleeping Place (destroyed)
1973
Plaster, linen
60 × 76 × 152 cm

It can be argued that Gormley's initial quest was for intellectual knowledge and understanding of the world around him; he worked with objects which were cut open or flayed – skins were subtracted. At first, nothing was hidden; subsequently, as objects came to be covered – skins added – nothing was revealed. And although it was only a short step, in formal terms, from the enclosure of objects in sheets of lead to the encasing of bodies in the same material, this focus of attention on the figure coincided with a radical shift in the artist's

priorities: it reflected a growing desire to embody experience rather than knowledge. Gormley had decided to explore, in sculpture, what it feels like to be human, to create images that mirrored states of being.

Many of the artist's drawings provide an especially keen sense of Gormley's experience of 'innerliness': they suggest that man can be seen just as clearly with the inner eye as with the outer, and that within the container of the skin lies a world of polarities, oppositions and a plethora of feelings and emotions. In Gormley's drawings bodies freefloat, as if in a womb or in outer space; they interact with each other and yet still remain fundamentally alone. They also appear to have overcome the division between body and spirit.

The impression that Gormley's view of inner space is more fluid and expansive than his perception of outer reality is corroborated by a number of lead pieces made during the mid-1980s. *Tree* and *Field*, for example, which were direct translations from drawings, are simultaneously fantastic and uncanny. (Commenting on the elongated limbs and necks of such pieces, Gormley has said, 'To make concrete the life that goes on inside the head one can't stay within classic proportions'[32]). And *Present Time*, in which two headless body cases are joined at the neck – one is upside down, with arms outstretched and legs slightly astride, the other, on the ground, is tautly self-contained – has the disorienting effect of true surrealism. *Mind* similarly encapsulates the paradoxes that flow from this position: it is evocative of an enlarged, floating brain and, besides, of a small, leaden cloud.

Earth
1994
Ink on paper
14 × 19.5 cm

Into
1994
Ink on paper
14 × 19.5 cm

Field
1984-85
Lead, fibreglass, plaster, air
195 × 560 × 66 cm

Rearranged Desert
1979
Death Valley
before, A centrally placed cairn
made of stone cleared from a
circular area, the radius being the
distance of a hand-sized stone
flung as far as possible;
during, Throwing the stones as far
as possible in all directions from
the central cairn;
after, Rearranged Desert

But Gormley has also – and strongly – been drawn to the outside world, usually as part of a quest to find correspondences to his experience of inner space. Among his early pieces were a work, constructed with sticks in the mouth of a cave in Greece (revealingly, he has described this as an attempt to 'reactivate its interior') and another, called *Rearranged Desert*, that he made in Arizona. The latter, in which he 'tested' the boundaries of his reach by throwing stones as far as he could, involved the 'relocation of earth' – a process that was both literal and symbolic, as one of Gormley's basic principles is that everything that exists, including man, can be defined as 'earth above ground'. It was also an echo, in a different context, of the idea he expressed in the drawing *Exercise between Blood and Earth*.

Since then, Gormley's search for correlatives to the expansiveness of inner space has led to the siting of many pieces in unusual architectural settings and in the landscape. Their locations have been varied, ranging from a plaza in Rennes, to the flooded crypt of Winchester Cathedral to the city walls of Derry (see page 81), and, most recently, to an ambitious project in a Norwegian fjord (see page 11). (In placing work in these locations, Gormley seems to be inviting the community at large, and not just the individual, to 'inhabit' their inner spaces.)

(see page 81)

(see page 11)

Open Space
1994
Body case, iron, 46 x 105 x 36 cm
Disc, concrete, diam. 30 m
Public commission in La Place
Jean-Monnet, Rennes, France

opposite, **Sound II**
1986
Lead, fibreglass, water
188 × 60 × 45 cm
Collection, Winchester Cathedral

above, **Sculpture for Derry Walls**
(detail)
1987
Cast iron, three double figures
196 × 193 × 54 cm

top right, **Sculpture for Derry
Walls** (detail showing
vandalization with burnt tyres)

opposite, **Room for the Great
Australian Desert**
1989
Concrete
92 × 58 × 51 cm

symbolized his wish to maintain contact with
the outside world. This box, a concentrated and
simplified form, as Anthony Bond put it, 'articulates
the focussing potential of man in the land'[34]. At the
same time, many miles away in the Gallery in New
South Wales, he placed 1,100 figurines, made from
clay drawn from the same pans in the centre of
Australia. Each one, individually fashioned, was
unique. Positioned in two hemispheres around
a central path that crossed the Gallery space
diagonally, they were spaced most densely near
the centre of the room and radiated out like the
lines of force of a magnetic field. The viewer,
inevitably attracted to the centre of the space,
was then positioned in the middle of a field of
energy, surrounded by figures with upraised eyes.

While earlier work, such as *Rearranged Desert*
or the many body cases set in outside locations,
seemed to focus on the potential transformative
power of human presence, the *Room* created an
awareness of the massive, and threatening, energy
of the earth. The concrete casing and the crouched
figure within it were as nothing compared to the
emptiness of the desert; inner space, hitherto
conceived as infinite, could be perceived as more
confining than the potential of the outside world.
In contrast, the embodied viewer, positioned at the
centre of *Field*, was made to feel vastly greater than
the fragile figurines, all of whom gaze upwards, as
if in supplication. Taken together, these pieces
reflect a new spirit of openness, humility, and a
willingness to accept the responsibility of being a
fallible human in a material world.

But besides the installation at Charleston
Old Jail, possibly Gormley's most complete
exploration of the complexities of space can be
found in two parallel works he made in 1989.
These pieces, driven by the artist's conviction
that 'if we are to survive we must balance outer
action with the inner experience of matter'[33], are
A Room for the Great Australian Desert, and *Field for
the Art Gallery of New South Wales*. Here, as in the
early *Full Bowl*, Gormley succeeded in eliminating
the boundary between inner and outer space.

On a flat expanse of red dust and clay pans
in central Australia, Gormley placed a concrete
box – a container proportioned in such a way
that it could accommodate the figure of a man
crouching on the ground with his knees close to
his chest. The two-inch shell was closed, except
for four orifices – ears, mouth, and penis – which

above, **Field for the Art Gallery of
New South Wales**
1989
Terracotta
23 × 1140 × 1050 cm

Untitled (for Francis)
1986
Lead, fibreglass, plaster
188 × 119 × 34 cm
Installed, Maenz Psychiatric
Clinic, Germany
Collection, Tate Gallery, London

VI

There is a steady rhythm to the development of
Antony Gormley's art; the whole body of work
breathes. Some pieces suggest inner expansion,
as though they are the result of in-breaths; others
have the generosity and breadth of exhalation.
Broadly speaking, the lead body cases are like
inhalations, while the works in clay are more
effusive. What makes the difference is the 'skin'
of the piece the skin being the threshold, or
boundary, that both describes and identifies
the subject.

If the impetus behind the body cases reflected
the artist's determination to discover his own most
fundamental responses to the world, uncluttered by
the business of thinking, this withdrawal from the
movement of the mind also signalled a certain
isolationism. (Sometimes their 'existential'
aloneness can be reminiscent of the sculpture of
Giacometti.) Their contemplative stillness, like that
of deep concentration or meditation, maintained
distance from the chaos of the everyday world, as if
to preserve a living and vulnerable being in a state
of quiescence. Most of the lead cases are silent and
sealed; the energy they contain is inaccessible.

But many of the body cases are perforated.
Some, like *Three Ways*, have holes that correspond to
the body's orifices, which suggest interaction
between the outside world and the presence within
the leaden skins. In others, such as *Untitled (for
Francis)*, the eye-shaped holes look like wounds, or
stigmata. One work in particular, *Sovereign State*,
brings both these characteristics together. Gormley
describes its conception as follows: 'I wanted to
make an image of power deposed. Of a king pushed

to the floor, lying next to his support mechanism
which echoes his biological internal mechanism.
In expanding the body case, it began to look like
an astronaut's suit. In destroying the hierarchy
between the stratosphere and the earth, between
the king and his subjects, one of the principle
transitions of the work is to make the viewer himself
the subject of the work, and that is also part of the
sovereignty that the work depicts'[35].

While *Sovereign State* is the most complete
example of the breakdown of Gormley's belief in
the invulnerability and self-sufficiency embodied
by the lead cases, his works in concrete pieces are
also a manifestation of a growing desire to engage
with the world. As the artist has explained, 'the
block describes the space between the body and
a compressed notion of architecture, and what I
find makes them quite tender is that the principle
gesture of all those works is touch … The concrete
has become, as it were, a necessary conditionality.
The work has always identified the minimum space
necessary for a man to occupy, but I think the
concrete pieces do it in a more intimate, open,
and direct way. There is a real point of contact with
the particularity of my body – slipped from life into
art, with every wrinkle of the knuckles embedded in
the concrete'[36].

There is a shift of emphasis, too, which is
reflected by Gormley's increased use of iron
instead of lead, and especially by his 'expansion'
pieces. Iron, closer to earth than lead, responds
to changes in the atmosphere; it rusts, corrodes,
and eventually disintegrates. At the same time,
iron is solid and relatively impenetrable. And it is
significant that Gormley's use of cast-iron is at its

Sovereign State
1989-90
Brass, lead, plaster, fibreglass, air
rubber hose
Figure, 66 × 172 × 98 cm
Hose length, 30,000 cm

opposite
Sense
1991
Concrete
74.5 × 62.5 × 60cm

below
Flesh
1990
Concrete
36 × 198 × 174 cm

overleaf, l. to r.
Earth
1991-93
Cast iron, air
312 × 230 × 290 cm

Fruit
1991-93
Cast iron, air
104 × 125 × 120 cm

Body
1991-93
Cast iron, air
260 × 200 × 280 cm

most effective in the 'expansion' works, which hold within them, albeit invisibly, the imprint of the artist's body. In these pieces, as in the early drawing, *Exercise between Blood and Earth*, the body's 'energy-fields' have expanded to the point where they begin to resemble ripe fruits that can barely be contained within their skins. *Earth* and *Body* are like chrysalises: they are in transition, about to generate new life. And as Gormley once wrote about them, the 'expansion' pieces have much to do with 'mind and its sensibilities not fitting completely comfortably in the skin'[37].

Gormley's exploration of the idea of 'expansion' is most fully expressed in the works made of clay. Veit Loers has noted that, in the mid-1980s, the idea of transformation was dealt with narratively, adding

clay as a new creative element, also pointing out that this element was invisibly present as earth in the early *Three Bodies*[38]. And in pieces like *The Beginning, the Middle, and the End* and *Out of This World*, schematic terracotta figurines escape, unprotected, from their lead body cases.

That Gormley associates clay, or earth, with a sense of freedom is indicated in works as different as *Man Asleep* and *Room for the Great Australian Desert*, where the ground itself acts as an undifferentiated source of energy. It is in *Field*, however, that what Gormley has referred to as a 'return to desire' has its fullest expression, for if the lead body cases can plausibly be read as images of withdrawal from the chaos of the outer world into a state of still awareness or contemplation, *Field* could be said to be their opposite.

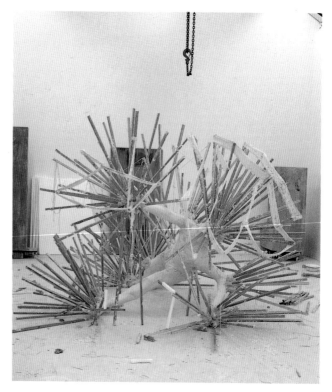

Still Leaping, in progress
1994
Plaster and iron cast
368 × 326 × 242 cm
Caldic Collection, the Hague

Brick Man (Model)
1987
Terracotta, fibreglass, plaster
196 × 50 × 38 cm
Collection, Leeds City Art Gallery

Field is based on a simple idea: a group of people are brought together to work with earth and to create a collective body (in that respect it echoes the motivation behind Gormley's unrealized plan, to build a gigantic *Brick Man* in Leeds). The parameters within which the figurines are created are precise, yet unrestrictive: each one hand-sized and similar in proportion, but of necessity has its own character. They are a celebration of community, of everyday humanity; and when brought together en masse, with their eyes turned towards the thresholds of the spaces in which they are shown, they bring the viewer into the configuration as well. *Field*, like the rest of Gormley's work, causes the viewer to become self-aware – but, in this case, to be aware of the self as being immensely important and, simultaneously, only a minute part of the collective body of mankind.

Because it represents something close to the fulfilment of many of his artistic and ethical aspirations, the importance of this work in Gormley's artistic development can scarcely be overestimated. Having rejected its focus on the unique individual creator and the singular art object, *Field* breaks through the limitations of the Western sculptural tradition; it also, just as importantly, reflects a movement away from the self to dealing with others, and from making something finished to undertaking a task that will never be completed.

The tension between the 'self' and 'not-self' that characterizes the body-cases is resolved, in a most unexpected fashion, by *Field*. While the body-cases have a strong, self-contained beauty, in *Field*, as the artist has put it, 'placeness' has overcome 'objectness'[39]. It alludes to the intense fragility of the 'skin of living matter' and to the interconnectedness of life; it represents the 'invasion' of cerebral purity by the chaos of the earth, and of Western 'civilization' by 'the remote, the marginal, the dispossessed, the unacknowledged'[40]. It is reminiscent of Biblical stories about creation and the end of the world, just as it is evocative of the Buddhist doctrine of 'anatta' or 'no-Soul'.

Antony Gormley's personal and artistic ambition, which is nothing less than the transformation of the individual and communal body, has found its most complete expression in these inchoate masses of terracotta figurines, made by hands other than his own. *Field*, as the artist has remarked, accommodates two factors: 'the spirit of the ancestors; the primal population made of the earth, where mud takes on the attributes of sentience and the evocation of the unborn – those who are yet to come'[41]. And perhaps the reason why these works are so affecting is because *Field* is a landscape of gazes, 'which look to us to find their place'[42]. And the figurines, almost uniquely in the body of Gormley's sculpture, are possessed of eyes, the outward expression of insight.

1 Quoted in Ananda K. Coomaraswamy, *The Transformation of Nature in Art*, Dover, New York, 1956, p. 76

2 Ibid., p. 95

3 Interview with Roger Bevan in catalogue, *Learning to See*, Galerie Thaddaeus Ropac, Paris; Salzburg, 1993, p. 38

4 Catalogue, *Places with a Past*, Rizzoli International, New York, 1991, p. 120

5 Ibid., p. 123

6 Ibid., p. 123

7 Ibid., p. 124

8 Quoted in Richard Kearney, *Poetics of Imagining*, HarperCollins Academic, London, 1991, p. 114

9 The philosopher, Jean-Luc Nancy, develops this idea in *The Birth to Presence*, Stanford University Press, California, 1993, p. 192.

10 '(The) attitude of man struggling against the forces of nature ... to impose an order through understanding (of a particular kind) is the attitude that created the enlightenment and the Newtonian world view. Descartes' Cogito is the opposition of the mind to the world – my job is to reintegrate it'. Interview with Ewa Ayton, *Art and Business*, Warsaw, March/April 1994, p. 75

11 Nancy, op. cit., p. 191

12 Nicholas Serota, introduction to *Transformations: New Sculpture from Britain*, British Council, London, 1983, p. 10

13 Lynne Cooke, essay in catalogue, *Antony Gormley*, Salvatore Ala Gallery, New York, 1984

14 Interview with Ewa Ayton, op. cit., p. 75

15 Stephen Bann, 'The Raising of Lazarus', in catalogue, *Antony Gormley*, Malmö Konsthall; Tate Gallery, Liverpool; Irish Museum of Modern Art, Dublin, 1993, p. 40

16 Stephen Bann, 'Sculpture/Interpretation: The Space Outside and The Space Inside', unpublished lecture, 1994

17 Michael Newman, 'Antony Gormley's Drawings', in catalogue, *Gormley*, Seibu Contemporary Art Gallery, Tokyo, 1987, n.p.

18 Shearer West, *Fin de Siècle – Art and Society in an Age of Uncertainty*, Bloomsbury, London, 1993. This book was drawn to the writer's attention by Antony Gormley.

19 James Hall, 'Frame Game', *The Guardian*, London, 7 November, 1994

20 C.G. Jung, as well as the Jungian analyst, Marie-Louise von Franz, have written extensively on the subject.

21 The former is described, the latter illustrated, in Marie-Louise von Franz, *Alchemy*, Inner City Books, Toronto, 1980.

22 Mary Douglas, *Purity and Danger*, Pelican, Harmondsworth, 1966, p. 210

23 Interview with Ewa Ayton, op. cit., p. 71

24 Stephen Bann raises this issue in his unpublished lecture, 'Sculpture/Interpretation: The Space Outside and the Space Inside'.

25 Interview with Declan McGonagle, in catalogue, *Antony Gormley*, Malmö Konsthall; Tate Gallery Liverpool; Irish Museum of Modern Art, Dublin, 1993, pp. 44-45

26 Lewis Biggs, 'Learning to See – an Introduction', ibid., p. 25

27 Interview with Declan McGonagle, op. cit., p. 46

28 Mary Douglas, op. cit., p. 210

29 Antony Gormley, slide/tape presentation

30 Stuart Morgan, 'The Genesis of Secrecy', in *Transformations – New Sculpture from Britain*, British Council, London, 1983, p. 42

31 Ibid.

32 Quoted in Sandy Nairne, 'Such Stuff as Dreams are Made of', in catalogue, *Antony Gormley*, Stadtische Galerie, Regensburg; Kunstverein, Frankfurt, 1985, p. 58

33 Antony Gormley interviewed by Anthony Bond, in the catalogue, *A Field for the Art Gallery of New South Wales, A Room for the Great Australian Desert*, Art Gallery of New South Wales, Sydney, 1989, n.p.

34 Ibid.

35 Interview with Declan McGonagle, op. cit., p. 47

36 Ibid., p. 51

37 Letter from Antony Gormley to the writer, 27 August 1994

38 Veit Loers, 'Calling upon Matter', in the catalogue, *Antony Gormley*, Stadtische Galerie, Regensburg; Frankfurter Kunstverein, 1985, p. 42

39 Interview with Marjetica Potrc, in the catalogue, *Field for the British Isles*, Oriel Mostyn, Llandudno, Wales, 1994, p. 61

40 Ibid., p. 73

41 Ibid., p. 62

42 Ibid., p. 62

Contents

overleaf
European Field
Terracotta
approx. 35,000 figures, 8-26 cm
each
Installed, Konsthall Malmö

opposite
**American Field, Forming a
figurine**
December, 1990
St. Mathias, Cholula Mexico

It's raining. At noon I step from the bus, into a puddle which surrounds the entrance to the main Post Office, at the busiest bus stop in Ljubljana; whether people want to make a call or send a letter, cross to the far end of the city or arrive in the central marketplace, go to the bank, or maybe just have an appointment for lunch at this, the beginning of the busiest hour of the day, they must all wade through it. The puddle is not a cavity full of water in the pavement at all, but jets of water spraying around the knees and bouncing off shoes; splashing off the pavement they look like barbed wire, here, on the busiest corner in Ljubljana.

Even though I wear rubber boots, my feet are soaked as I stand at the crossroads, waiting for the green light. A street stretches out in front of me, so straight that where it climbs a hill in the park, I can see, despite the motley crowds in the foreground, a very short and a very thin, white gravel line, that leads above their heads, to the mansion. The sky becomes brighter, it turns from grey into blue, the colours still cold, the sun not yet broken through the canopy of clouds.

A flood of people tows me on, a lady with her shopping bag filled to bursting pushes me and I hold my long umbrella close, so as not to pierce her bag. As I walk across the street the wind starts blowing. Droplets on my calves turn cold. I wipe them away as I pass the shop-windows and avoid the people, who loiter in front of them. I do not manage to wipe myself dry because the thin web of my stockings keeps the water on my skin; my feet are damp and my stockings wet. At ground level I feel unpleasantly cold.

There are fewer and fewer people and more and more daylight around me as I walk out of the town centre. The building of the Opera becomes, no longer ochre, but yellow. The beige ornaments on its facade become white. The buildings are lower and don't eat the sky away any more; the sky has become completely blue. Even the pavement is drier and beneath it, by the side of the road, there is a little puddle which is absolutely smooth, waiting for the wheel of a car.

I run obstinately towards it. I poke it with the tip of my umbrella and stir it, so that the water rises up into the air and falls back splashing, although it does not leap even as high as my ankles. 'Hey, no more wet feet', I say to myself.

I turn my back on the gazes of the passers-by and walk across the street again. There is nobody on this side. I stop at the beginning of the gravel pathway which now seems

American Field, Figures drying
December, 1990
St. Mathias, Cholula Mexico

broader than the distance between the finger-tips of my outstretched arms.

It is impossible to see the mansion because it is blocked by a concrete bridge over which runs a railway. The hill looks like the lid of a pot placed over the bridge's iron railings. The forest, burdened under the weight of the rain which is still in the tree-tops, spreads over the hill; a blueness flutters over it caressing me with its soft light.

The only day of the week when the Ljubljana natives can stroll around here is Sunday. This is when they take time out for nature, God or art. If it wasn't for this a taste for adventure might remain unappeased. I turn left into the Museum of Modern Art and here I am, having passed the porter, alone again. I want to see the little statues that the English sculptor is exhibiting here. 'In the show-room at the end', the porter directs me. Familiar with the place, I boldly proceed, but am forced, immediately, to stop. From one wall to the other, right up to the door, the large room is filled with thousands of simians no taller than two palms of a hand. Their bodies are formless bulks that are burned through; their heads are raised and together, they fix on me with their cavities, two holes that pierce me inside more unavoidably than any kind of look.

These figurines form a field, which, with a forbidding power, deflects the visitor's attention away from their fragility, and onto his or her inner being. My defensive stare in the face of this confrontation with this crowd of repeated forms becomes a weapon, which turns on me. In front of me there is a light which I can feel. It is not as rapturous as it was outside, but it glows, the motionless, luminous guardian of a reddish army which stands to attention.

inside me, where my tongue touches the roof of my mouth, is the pad of taste. it is cold and smooth. it feels metallic and sticky, so that my tongue cannot move. saliva accumulates under it and pours like a tide across it as far as my throat. the foam of saliva neutralises the acidity of the spot where my palate is corroding my tongue. the taste in my mouth was not caused by fruit which my teeth would crush, so that's why it isn't sour; the taste in my mouth is not a trace of soup, which would slide down my throat, which is why it isn't salty; the taste is the lesion of time, bent into the mould of my body, a body made vulnerable by the constant assault of time.

time, confined into blind caves or extended through tunnels, responds to the call of infinity, which teases with its promise of freedom. outside the body, time is a pair of compasses in the hands of eternity, but inside it is a pendulum, fastened to the heart. the heart takes its measure from the lengthening swing of the pendulum surveying what time is left. in its own rhythm time spreads itself wildly here and there and is crippled elsewhere. its unequally distributed weight wounds my body - that is how the particularities of my life are manifest.

my body sustains many injuries, it is furrowed by the fluids I secrete, the air that

European Field (detail)
1993
Terracotta
approx. 35,000 figures, 8-26 cm each
Installed, Malmö Konsthall

time sucks into me. my inner being is so corroded that it is as if it was turned inside out. only the vessel of flesh models the space into a form that looks like me. in the beginning the body moves towards the other, full of an expectant pulse. but the rhythm of blood becomes increasingly more convulsive. the procedures of osmosis make the body expel the blood from the shelter it seeks. i am drawn into the infinite procedures of removal. fatally attracted, my body is swallowed up, transformed, so that sinews become unentwined from the supple bands that exchange substances. they stop responding to stimulation and atrophy turns to alabaster.

time insinuates itself into all that exists. fragments shaped by the particularities of existence are united by the seal of sameness. that is why i cannot restore my body as a border. time occupies the body, consuming and chiselling it into patterns of transition.

the lesion of metallic stickiness in my mouth becomes as heavy as lead and forces my tongue back into my throat. the heart guards this opening as the only exit among the many doors of the body. between two lives which are linked together - the eternal and the transitory - the mouth is a safety valve which stops one rejecting the other. language, a form which eternity alone is unable to create, passes through the mouth into the world.

European Field
1994
Terracotta
approx. 35,000 figures, 8-26 cm
each
Installed, Muzej Surremene
Umjetnosh, Zagreb

The fist in which I've been squeezing my umbrella starts prickling. I change hands and loosen up my knees; I've been standing bolt upright all this time. I lean on my right leg and start feeling a mellow relief in the muscles of the left one. In front of me the figures become more prominent against the light. The statuettes are no longer a compact mass of earth that won't allow me in, pitting their thousands of eye cavities against me. In spite of the resistant pressure of their gaze, I endured, transcended their otherness and entered their space. The threat evoked by their stillness has disappeared. I obeyed their imperative, to enter myself; I watched them from inside.

The flames have sublimated the individual litheness of each figure so that together they make even the light gleam; it confronts and combines with the presence of the morning rain its footsteps still visible on my overcoat. The army from the stove has lost its vigilance and gained the mellowness of grapes spread out after the vintage. My foot could not harm these heads now. I was ready to undergo their process of becoming, to burn myself to the core. The clay is becoming blue in colour. As if it is sharing, with me, a need to leave this box, and return to open space.

As I am leaving, the rubber of my boots squeaks on the parquet. The porter is already waiting for me so he can close the Museum. At the top of the stairs before the exit I spot a brown dachshund no taller than two palms of a hand, as he pokes his snout inside. The door slams behind me, the dachshund jumps back and runs away, even though the rain is coming down from the sky again. Yet the sky doesn't become grey, its massed clouds make it soft and it stays sky-blue. I do not use the umbrella against this rain. Instead of returning to the town, I turn to the wood. In a shelter under the railway bridge the dachshund stops. His powerful, penetrating look reminds me of the unexpected reception in the Museum, but he quickly loses interest in me. With his ears poking forward he drifts off, waving me away with his very short and very thin white tail. As he disappears, I wade through the first puddle and slowly, scraping its bottom, watch how the waves lap one against the other just like a storm at sea. This is happening low, low around my boots, not reaching my legs at all.

Contents

VIII

And so I come to the fields and vast palaces of memory, where are stored the innumerable images of material things brought to it by the senses. Further there is stored in the memory the thoughts we think, by adding to or taking from or otherwise modifying the things that sense has made contact with, and all other things that have been entrusted to and laid up in memory, save such as forgetfulness has swallowed in its grave. When I turn to memory, I ask it bring forth what I want: and some things are produced immediately, some take longer as if they had to be brought out from some more secret place of storage; some pour out in a heap, and while we are actually wanting and looking for something quite different, they hurl themselves upon us in masses as though to say: 'May it not be we that you want?' I brush them from the face of my memory with the hand of my heart, until at last the thing I want is brought to light as from some hidden place. Some things are produced just as they are required, easily and in right order; and things that come first give place to those that follow, and giving place are stored up again to be produced when I want them. This is what happens, when I say anything by heart.

In the memory all the various things are kept distinct and in their right categories, though each came into the memory by its own gate. For example, light and all the colours and shapes of bodies come in by the eyes, all the kinds of sound by the ears, all scents by the nostrils, all tastes by the mouth; and by a sense that belongs to the whole body that comes in what is hard and what is soft, what is hot or cold, rough or smooth, heavy or light, whether outside the body or inside. All these things the vast recesses, the hidden and unsearchable caverns, of memory receive and store up, to be available and brought to light when need arises: yet all enter by their own various gates to be stored up in memory. Nor indeed do the things themselves enter: only the images of the things perceived by the senses are there for thought to remember them.

And even though we know by which senses they were brought in and laid up in the memory, who can tell how these images were formed? Even when I am in darkness and in silence, I can if I will produce colours in my memory, and distinguish black from white and any other colours if I choose; and sounds do not break in and disturb the image I am considering that came in through the eye, since the sounds themselves were already there and lie stored up apart. For I can summon them too, if I like, and they are immediately present; and though my tongue is at rest and my throat silent I can sing as I will; nor do the images of the colours, although they are as truly present, interfere or interrupt when I call from the storehouse some other thing which came in by the ear. Similarly all other things that were brought in by the other senses and stored up in the memory can be called up at my pleasure: I distinguish the scent of lilies from the scent of violets, though at that instant I smell nothing; and I like honey better than wine, some smooth thing better than rough, though I am not tasting or handling but only remembering.

Holding onto the Future
1987-88
Cast iron, air
74 × 174 × 87 cm

Three Ways: Mould, Hole and
Passage
1981
Lead, fibreglass, plaster
foreground,
Mould, 60 × 98 × 50 cm
middleground,
Hole, 62 × 123 × 80 cm
background,
Passage, 34 × 209 × 50 cm

All this I do inside me, in the huge court of my memory. In my memory are sky and earth and sea, ready at hand along with all the things that I have ever been able to perceive in them and have not forgotten. And in my memory too I meet myself - I recall myself, what I have done, when and where and in what state of mind I was when I did it. In my memory are all the things I remember to have experienced myself or to have been told by others. From the same store I can weave into the past endless new likenesses of things either experienced by me or believed on the strength of things experienced; and from these again I can picture actions and events and hopes for the future; and upon them all I can mediate as if they were present. 'I shall do this or that,' I say to myself in the vast recess of my mind with its immeasurable store of images of things so great: and this or that follows. 'O, if only this or that could be!' or again, 'May God prevent this or that!' Such things I say within myself, and when I speak of them the images of all the things I mention are to hand from the same storehouse of memory, and if the images were not there I could not so much as speak of the things.

Great is this power of memory, exceedingly great, O my God, a spreading limitless room within me. Who can reach its uttermost depth? Yet it is a faculty of my soul and belongs to my nature. In fact I cannot totally grasp all that I am. Thus the mind is not large enough to contain itself: but where can that part of it be which it does not contain? [How can there be any of itself that is not in itself?] As this question struck me, I was overcome with wonder and almost stupor. Here are men going afar to marvel at the heights of mountains, the mighty waves of the sea, the long courses of great rivers, the vastness of the ocean, the movements of the stars, yet leaving themselves unnoticed and not seeing it as marvellous that when I spoke of all these things, I did not see them with my eyes, yet I could not have spoken of them unless these mountains and waves and rivers and stars which I have seen, and the ocean of which I have heard, had been inwardly present to my sight: in my memory, yet with the same vast spaces between them as if I saw them outside me. When I saw them with my eyes, I did not by seeing them swallow them into me; nor are they themselves present in me, but only their images; and I know by what sense of my body each one of them was impressed upon my mind.

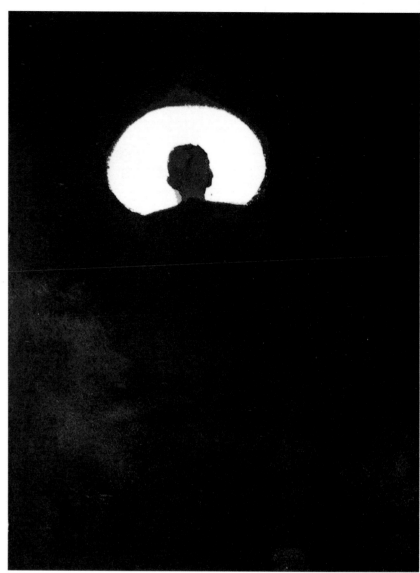

Baring Light III
1990
Plaster, fibreglass, lead,
rubber, air
16 × 41 × 27 cm

XVI

I can also name forgetfulness and know what I mean by the word; but how should I recognize the thing itself unless I remembered it? I am not speaking of the sound of the word, but of the thing the sound signifies; for if I had forgotten the thing, I should be unable to remember what the sound stood for. When I remember memory my memory itself is present to itself by itself; but when I remember forgetfulness, then memory and forgetfulness are present together - forgetfulness which I remember, memory by which I remember. But what is forgetfulness except absence of memory? How then can that be present for me to remember, which when it is present means that I cannot remember? If what we remember we hold in our memory, and if, unless we remembered forgetfulness, we should not on hearing the word recognize what is meant by it, then forgetfulness is contained in the memory. Therefore that is present, to keep us from forgetting it, which when it is present we do forget. Are we to understand from this that when we remember forgetfulness, it is not present to the memory in itself but by its image: because if it were present in itself it would cause us not to remember but to forget? Who can analyze this, or understand how it can be?

Assuredly, Lord, I toil with this, toil within myself: I have become to myself a soil laborious and of heavy sweat. For I am not now considering the parts of the heavens, or measuring the distances of the stars, or seeking how the earth is held in space; it is I who remember, I, my mind. It is not remarkable if things that I am not are far from my knowledge: but what could be closer to me than myself? Yet the power of memory in me I do not understand, though without memory I could not even name myself. What am I to say, when I see so clearly that I remember forgetfulness? Am I to say that something I remember is not in my memory? Or am I to say that forgetfulness is in my memory to keep me from forgetting? Either would be absurd. Is there a third possibility? Could I say that the image of forgetfulness is retained in my memory, not forgetfulness itself, when I remember it? But how could I say this since if the image of a thing is imprinted on the memory, the thing itself must first have been present, for the image to be able to be imprinted? Thus I remember Carthage and such other places as I have been in; I remember the faces of men I have seen and things reported by the other senses; I remember the health or sickness of the body. For when these were present, the memory received their images from them, and these remained present to be gazed on and thought about by the mind when in their absence I might choose to remember them. It follows that if forgetfulness is retained in the memory by means of an image and not in itself, then itself must at some time have been present for its image to be received. But when it was present, how did it write its image in my memory since by its presence it destroys what it finds noted there? At any rate whatever the manner of it, however incomprehensible and inexplicable, I am certain that I do remember forgetfulness, although by forgetfulness what we remember is effaced.

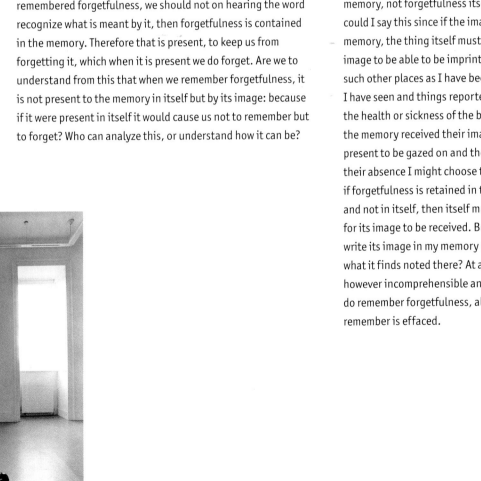

... on the ethnographical
... displays of the ...
... of the byzantine ...
... Tartars, Etc with
... sheepskin clothes,
... black jackets:
... like ukrainian
... was so many ...
... The three biggest ...
... benches — all
...

Contents

Glass Pool
1978
Glass
182 cm diam.
h. 8 mm

Skin V
1979
Sarsen stone
91 × 121 × 45 cm

To act in time and be acted on by time.

On the threshold, the works are gifts of the products of nature and culture to each other.
They are an attempt to stop time and re-present the world. In revelation or insulation
there is no concern to make things stand for anything other than what they are.

Open Door
1975
Wooden door
206 × 206 × 8 cm

Floor
1981
Rubber
122 × 91 × 1 cm

Artist's Writings

left, **Proof**
1984
Lead, fibreglass, plaster, air
80 × 56 × 80 cm

Things already exist.
Sculpture already exists.

The job is to transform what exists in the outer world
by uniting it with the world of
sensation, imagination and faith.

Action can be confused with life.
Much of human life is hidden.
Sculpture, in stillness, can transmit what may not be seen.

My work is to make bodies into vessels
that both contain and occupy space.

Space exists outside the door and inside the head.

My work is to make a human space in space.

Each work is a place between form and formlessness,
a time between origin and becoming.

A house is the form of vulnerability,
darkness is revealed by light.

My work is to make a place, free from knowledge,
free from history, free from nationality to be experienced freely.

In art there is no progress, only art.
Art is always for the future.

October, 1985, published in *Antony Gormley: Five Works* (cat.),

Serpentine Gallery, London; Arts Council of Great Britain, London, 1987

opposite
left, **Dark**
1986
Lead, fibreglass, plaster, air
100 × 100 × 120 cm
right, **12 Hours: The Beginning,
the Middle, the End**
1985-86
Lead, fibreglass, plaster, air
23 × 28 × 840 cm

Concerning the Religious Dimension in My Art 1987

Concerning the religious dimension in my art:

The work comes from the same source as the need for religion: wanting to face existence and discover meaning. The work attempts by starting with a real body in real time to face space and eternity. The body – or rather the place that the body occupies is seen as the locus on which those forces act.

Concerning death in the work:

I see all 'things' as earth above ground. We are the most vertical animal. We have been made conscious by space and are full of space. Space exists within us as imagination, thought and sensation and outside of us in terms of distance. Death is a doorway. For me it is an affirmation of the mystery of life and connects in some way with our nature as space. I see space in light and in darkness; one has to do with the imagination and the other with thought.

Culture and our bodies:

I do believe in stressing the physical aspect of consciousness because I believe that is what connects us as human beings. For me there are two kinds of culture, one that is an expression of the connection of man with the physical world that surrounds him and the other is familiar to us all as Western rationalization that separates us from the physical world. The paradox of this is that one leads to materialism and rationalization and the other to magic and freedom. My job in a broken but self-conscious world is to reaffirm connection. The world and my body I must identify as one.

Unpublished notebook entry

r, air
38.5 × 108 × 196 cm

Standing Ground
1986-87
Lead, fibreglass, plaster, air
193 × 191 × 35 cm

The Impossible Self (extract) 1988

Hold
1986
Lead, fibreglass, plaster, air
93 × 61 × 38.5 cm

Pore
1988
Lead, fibreglass, plaster, air
84 × 66 × 80 cm
Installed, Winnipeg Art Gallery,
Manitoba
Collection, Moderna Museet,
Stockholm

I think the whole history of man since the Enlightenment is one of control: of the world understood as an object out there, of vision requiring distance which promotes knowledge. My work tries to create a place of feeling, which is in contrast to objective rationalism.

I question the notion that retinal response is the only channel of communication in art, and the notion that objects are discrete entities. I want to work to activate the space around it and engender a psycho-physical response, allowing those in its field of influence to be more aware of their bodies and surroundings.

It is necessary these days to hold on to the crucial function art has in the continuance and regulation of life. It provides us with images and acts by which we identify ourselves but so often now in an unstable way. Art can be a focus for life by reasserting in times of vicissitude the central beliefs of a people. In tribal cultures it is a collective act whether in dance, carving, self-decoration that reasserts the body of the people and it is from this that the individual draws his or her power. Art and the practice of nonutilitarian skills is an act of will for the future and is as critical an aspect of survival as hunting or gathering food. What has happened to this urgency expressed in a collective creativity that projects into the future and ensures the belief necessary for life? It is not that we have lost it, but the repositories of dance, dream and art are dispersed into the hands of individuals who have responsibility not simply to a single family or tribe but as points of consciousness of the whole world.

The Impossible Self (cat.), Winnipeg Art Gallery, Manitoba, 1988

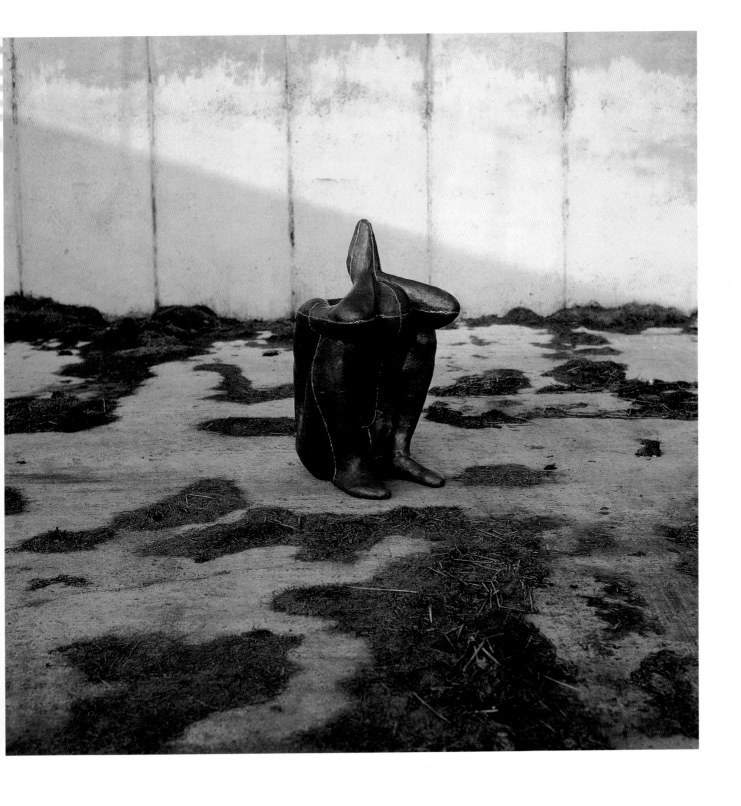

Being the World 1989

opposite, **Immersion**
1991
Concrete
181 × 50.5 × 36.5 cm

overleaf, **Natural Selection**
(details)
1981
Lead tools, fruit, weapons,
vegetables, objects
Dimensions variable
Collection, Tate Gallery, London

Nature is within us. We are sick when we do not feel it. The sickness of feeling separate from the world is what is killing it. We are earth above ground, clothed by space, seen by light. The distance inherent in sight has made us treat the 'outside' as different. The dominance of reason depends on the continued externalisation of the world. The light of reason is balanced by the darkness of the body. The unknownness of the mind and the unknownness of the universe are the same. If we are to survive, we must balance outer action with an inner experience of matter. This is the great subjectivity and the great unity. This unity is expressed by those who live close to the earth in living ways. We must integrate our perceptions of the dynamic interpenetration of the elements with the workings of the mind and realise them in the workings of the body. We must become consciously unconscious and unconsciously conscious. We are the world, we are the poisoners of the world, we are the consciousness of the world.

A Field for the Art Gallery of New South Wales, A Room for the Great Australian Desert (cat.), Art Gallery of New South Wales, Sydney, 1989

Refuge
1985
Lead, fibreglass, air
172 × 46 × 46 cm

Seeds IV
1993
Lead
Unit size, l. 3.5, diam. 1.1 cm

Learning to See: Body and Soul 1992

Untitled (Penis), from 'Body and Soul'
1990
Etching
30 × 40 cm

Untitled (Fingers), from 'Body and Soul'
1990
Etching
30 × 40 cm

If late modernist painting conflated the figure and the ground in the interests of a single unequivocal surface, I propose that the body is the ground and that at the other side of appearance is a space far greater than the space against which, traditionally, the body is figured. If Caspar David Friedrich's *Monk and the Sea* is a Rothko with a man in it, I am trying to make a case for a man containing the boundless space of consciousness.

I know all of this is in profound opposition to the post-modern sign-reading, language-orientated currencies, but I hope neither in any nostalgic nor negative way. Perhaps I feel that the world out there is getting pretty good at interpreting itself as we are sold images of ourselves from soaps on television to knitwear ads on the street and I want to explore something else – it's as if the sophistication of culture feeding on culture has left Being out.

Being is rather a vague term. What I am asking is rather than Being engaged with acting in the world, is it possible to express consciousness with no object but itself? Being contained in the body and its feelings, Being conveyed as immersion, where questions of culture become irrelevant.

We have long considered art objects as things in the world. Minimal self-referentiality has been replaced by an enjoyment of judging an object's relation to other objects. In a deconstructive world, art objects have become part of the deconstructing process and a reflection of the plurality of languages and the relativism of value.

I still like the essentializing tendency of modernism because it is a way of feeling more alive. The problem with it was that it all got channelled into finding an objective formal language. I propose an absolute subjectivity allowing existence to become the material, subject and generating principle of art. This is an essentializing process but turned towards internal balance and survival; towards intrinsic value.

This exhibition brings together two works, *Body and Soul*: a series of nine etchings which I made between February and September 1990, and the sculpture *Learning to See* made in 1991. They are both works that evoke the deep space of the interior of the body. In the sculpture for the first time I have kept the lead-covered mould very close to my body and indicated the eyes looking within. I hope its held breath conveys a feeling of the infinity that consciousness inhabits and that you feel included in it. The etchings (my first) try to express touch as gravity made conscious and gravity as the attraction that binds us to the earth. The five dark plates are impressions of the five main orifices: a vision of the inner realm of the body irradiated by the light and energy of what Blake called 'the windows of the soul'.

Learning to See: Body and Soul (cat.), Contemporary Sculpture Centre, Tokyo, 1992

Untitled (Mouth), from 'Body and Soul' (detail)
1990
Etching
30 × 40 cm

Interview with Declan McGonagle (extract) 1993

Declan McGonagle You have used lead, concrete, iron and in *Host* in Charleston, river mud, to make sculpture. Where does material and its manipulation sit in your preoccupations as an artist?

Antony Gormley **At a certain stage I accepted the Buddhist position; I wanted to deny desire. I saw desire in some way as a false economy of art. The desire to aesthetically possess or be possessed. Hence for the last ten years the preoccupation with enclosing things in an aesthetically neutral material. I chose lead for the same reason as Maillol did for his nudes; he wanted to have a tension between the sensuality of the form and the distancing effect of the material. In about 1984 I realized that clay was an important material. There was a time just after I moved into the new studio when it was just full of clay and I was trying to find a way of making that wasn't imposing an image on the material but allowing a one-to-one relationship between my body and the body of the clay. The forms arose naturally from the space between my hands; clay was another way of dealing with the flesh. Out of this the very first ideas of the *Field* work came. I must have made several hundred before they had eyes and I then realized that eyes were life! Somehow that was a return to desire. With *Field*, joy in material contact is there: it is about touch and touch expressed for its own sake. Touch not just of my hands but of many people's hands. Gone was the feeling that in order to be serious there had to be extreme distance between the personal engendering of the work and its public showing.**

McGonagle It seems you did not allow yourself to enjoy the material, to be seduced or to exhibit that seduction in the final work, until recently. Did you find yourself getting to a point with the material and then deliberately distancing yourself?

Gormley **In the early 1980s I wanted my body to be the prime material. I didn't want the viewer to be seduced by the work for the wrong reasons, I wanted it to be a kind of objective appraisal of my relationship to the world. I am very aware that all dialectical thinking has limited use. We are setting up oppositions between unconditioned and conditioned attitudes but taking on the body was a desire to touch things deeper than at a dialectic level, which was different from a lot of my generation's attitudes to material and how material and meaning coalesce.**

McGonagle That sounds as if the distancing is possibly more than just material.

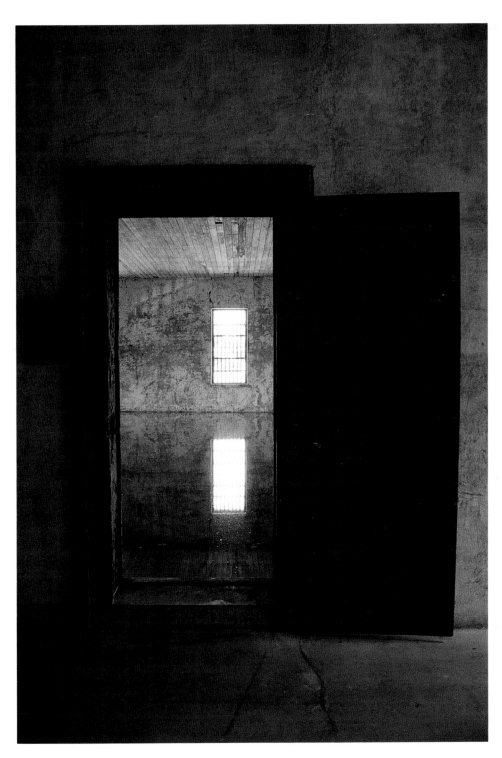

Host
1991
Mud, seawater
Depth 13 cm

Gormley I can well remember, at five or six, the first feeling of not belonging, and wondering whether I was really the son of my mother or father or whether I was some kind of implant. I think I had this sense from very early on (that I got from my father because he was always coming back from India, Malaya or Australia or somewhere) of there being another place where things were different, and that was the place for me.

From the moment I escaped from monastic education I was looking for another world view. I left the sacraments, and yet up to that point, Catholicism had been the central moral and life-supporting structure and remains a vital witness, because it is something that needs replacing. I need to build something as strong as that.

McGonagle Having had a religious, Catholic upbringing I recognize that impulse. Is your practice then built on the expression of anxiety rather than its resolution?

Gormley **What you recognize in the pieces in Derry and I recognize in *Field* (page 98-99) is a witnessing of our life but is in some sense also a judgement of it. A lot of the anxiety that I feel comes from the tensions between the chaos of daily life and the sense of judgement in the Catholic moral values with which I was indoctrinated at an early age. I was told as a child that I had the devil in me. Anxiety comes from feeling judged, from not being accepted. I want to start with things that just are, that cannot be judged because judgement does not alter them.**

McGonagle Do the works themselves enter the world as witnesses to this process, like *Close* as an idea but also in its siting?

Gormley **What I hope *Close* (page 61) does is test the notion of site as a fixed place with the idea that nothing is fixed. My work has been characterized as trying to carry on traditions of the transcendent or the utopian, but I'm not sure about that. I think what it tries to do is talk about some base in a very confusing world by confronting the earth. Because *Close* makes a relationship between itself and the earth, I think by implication the things that are on top of the earth in its vicinity are also implicated, and that includes the viewer.**

McGonagle So transcendental or utopian readings of your work are too easy?

Gormley **Yes I think it is an easy reading because it suggests that through the work there is an image of release and I think it's more like … the opposite.**

McGonagle Is it a doorway towards anxiety?

Gormley **I don't think it is that, either. There is a kind of collective madness that is taking us towards a terminal point, but there is also a feeling that this bodily existence of ours is only one level of existence. But I don't know what the next thing is, and the work doesn't pretend to know what the next thing is, either. All I'm trying to do is materialize the uncertainty, and to isolate some point of contact between consciousness and matter.**

McGonagle So all you can do is be here? Our human condition is about unknowing and uncertainty rather than knowing?

Home and the World
1985-86
Lead, fibreglass, wood,
plaster, air
57 × 405 × 55 cm

Gormley **Yes. I believe that whatever there is beyond is connected with what is here, and you can have a sense of dispersion of self when you sit for a while doing nothing but just being conscious of the body and feeling that attachment to body and self, me and mine disintegrate and you are able to experience energy rather than objects: that is freedom. Maybe people would call that death.**

McGonagle Have you described *Field* in the last few sentences?

Gormley **That's a very nice idea. The idea of being a place is rather like one consciousness being subsumed within a wider consciousness.**

McGonagle Would you make a distinction, then, between your use of the body and other current preoccupations with the body in the work of an artist like Kiki Smith, for instance, whom you feel sees the body as text?

Gormley **Yes, I think her interest in the body is, in a way, analytical, but I think what's great about the way that she uses that analysis is that she recognizes that the alimentary or neurological systems have a strong metaphoric meaning in terms of human society generally. But I still find the work plays on a peculiarly American phobia about the breakdown of the body or fear of disease – playing almost a doctoring role to that culture. I am not so concerned with recognition of the functions of the body. I am much more interested in the space that the body is. What is that space that you inhabit when you close your eyes?**

Kiki Smith
Virgin Mary
1992
Wax and pigment
Life-size

McGonagle It's interesting – this idea of work doctoring to a particular culture. Does your work doctor to any particular culture?

Gormley **'Doctor Heal Thyself', is more my line, and that means finding the other half of life that my upbringing excluded me from – which is an encounter with the earth, the body and the unconscious. You know my parents give me the initials AMDG (Ad Maiorem Dei Gloriam): For the Greater Glory of God. I can remember, when I was about six, my father taking me to one of the factories in his charge, when he had a foundation stone laid with AMDG on it, and a cross, and the date, and saying 'This is yours'.**

Seeing and Showing
1991-92
Lead, fibreglass, plaster
95 × 89 × 45 cm

McGonagle It must have looked like a tombstone.

Artist's Writings

Gormley **It did look like a tombstone. But the sense that the shape of my life was known somewhere else was something that I grew up with, and is both a limitation and a kind of enabler, because I don't think I would have set off at eighteen into the unknown without a guardian angel.**

McGonagle So is *A Case for an Angel* a declaration of faith?

Gormley **A *Case for an Angel* is a declaration of inspiration and imagination. It is an image of a being that might be more at home in the air, brought down to the earth. On the other hand it is also an image of somebody who is fatally handicapped, who cannot pass through any door and is desperately burdened. When installed it is a barrier across the space, blocking out the light and blocking the passage of the viewer. The top of the wings are actually at eye level and describe a kind of horizon beyond which you can't see very much, and so you feel trapped and there is a sense of an invitation to assert yourself in the space against it. It is an attempt to re-invent an idea of the object against which you can pit yourself, as in a Serra or a Judd, but differently.**

McGonagle Are you trying to draw upon a tradition or continuum which predates the Renaissance, which is pre-modern and still viable?

Gormley **Do you mean magic – how is that different from Modernism?**

McGonagle Well, the large scale exhibition at the Museum of Modern Art in 1984, '"Primitivism" and Twentieth Century Art', far from re-affirming the principles of Modernism, demonstrated its redundancy! To disconnect art from its social meaning, and value it only in terms of its formal properties, does a disservice to both the so-called 'primitive' practice and Modernist practice. Modernism (the idea that events result from human action) and magic (the pre-modern) may come in and out of focus in human history, but possibilities for both exist now. It's what makes this period particularly interesting, as we come to an end of particular values which ran from the Renaissance through the Reformation, the Enlightenment and nineteenth century Capitalism.

Gormley **There is a recuperation of both modernism and magic. This goes back to finding the other within. It's interesting in relation to the question: 'Is the work transcendent?'. *A Case for an Angel* is not ironic. I do believe that we can be transported or be the agent of** our own transcendence. Maybe transcendence is the wrong word – but the idea that flight, in gliding, depends on weight and its correct position, is fantastic. I like the marriage of anatomy and technology. It isn't a kind of Icarus – you know, little bird feathers. I want something that is very concrete. In terms of the idiom, you can see the technology and we know that it works. The expansion pieces are the opposite. They go the other way, and try to talk about the human extension into the organic world of cells and vegetables.

McGonagle You have said that the body is a collection of systems, that these systems can connect with other elemental systems.

Gormley **There are two ways of connecting with the elemental and one is technological and the other biological, and I think they are both valid, and both necessary. They both have to be made conscious – not extraction-orientated, integrational rather than exploitative and divisive.**

McGonagle But the body itself is quite muddled, isn't it?

Gormley **No, the body is the way it is. The mind is muddled. One's first relationship is with one's body. Then through one's body one begins to build up another kind of constellation of affection and, hopefully, an emerging sense of some kind of purpose. The sense of emerging purpose that a family describes has to be re-possessed as one of the points of resistance against the dispersal of self in consumer values.**

McGonagle You constantly use an image of dispersal in your discussion of the work, from individual pieces using lead, to the collective in *Field*, and now to the new iron work which is made up of several pieces.

Gormley **I'm thinking of calling the work *Testing a World View*. The work is a kind of psychological Cubism. An identical body cast made from the interior of a body case five times, which I then try to test against architecture. The piece expresses the polymorphousness of the self; that in different places we become different and I think this is physical. If Cubism is about taking one object and making multiple views of it in one place, this is a dispersion of one object into several cases for itself.**

left, **Richard Serra**
Olson
1985-86
Steel
Two plates,
288 × 1036.8 × 4.8 cm each

Donald Judd
Installation, Artillery sheds,
Chinati Foundation, Marfa, Texas
1993

overleaf, **Testing a World View**
1993
Cast iron
5 body cases,
each 1120 × 470 × 1180 cm

Artist's Writings

McGonagle Does it always have to be your own body?

Gormley I want to confront existence. It is obviously going to mean more if I use my own body. The optical and the conceptual have dominated in the art of the twentieth century and I turn to the body in an attempt to find a language that will transcend the limitations of race, creed and language, but which will still be about the rootedness of identity. It isn't just an idea about finding an idiom that could be universal, in a way that Modernism failed to do, it is an invitation to recognize a place and a base of consciousness. The body – I keep coming to this idea – is a moving sensor. I want the body to be a sensing mechanism, so your response to the work does not have to be pre-informed and does not necessarily encourage discourse. We are taught to use vision as an identifying force, which allied to discriminating intelligence fixes a thing. So that the strategy, for example, of Richard Deacon, deconstructing the physical world by suggesting multiple readings and denying any one in particular, is one possible strategy. But if you believe in subjects, which I do, you have to find another way. If my subject is being, somehow I have to manage to engage the whole being of the viewer.

I have always been bothered with the idea that the most visible bits of the Western figurative tradition of sculpture are dramatic muscular actions made in marble or bronze like the Discobolus, the Laokoon, or that fantastic Bernini work, *David*. What it suggests is that human potential can only be expressed sculpturally through the depiction of action. That moment of placing one foot in front of the other which began with the archaic Kouroi and continues with Michelangelo's *Slaves*, suggests that muscular action expresses the metaphysical tension between spirit and body, but I'm not so sure. Rodin momentarily recovered from that trap with his *Age of Bronze*; presenting a moment of becoming. What started as a heroic image of the soldier ends up being internalized and becomes a moment of self-consciousness within the body. For me this reconnects with the timelessness of pre-archaic Cycladic Greek sculpture which obviously uses the body in a completely different way as presence rather than actor. The head always addresses itself to the sky. There is something very powerful about the way that both Rodin's *Age of Bronze*, and the Cycladic heads connect being with the infinity of the sky, suggesting human potential, but not in terms of movement. I want to recapture that sense of imaginative space inside the body. I want there to be an internal pressure in the work, that has a relationship with the atmosphere which we sense with our bodies through the skin of the work.

Richard Deacon
If the Shoe Fits
1981
Galvanized corrugated steel,
screws
331 × 152 × 152 cm

McGonagle How else do you engage the viewer?

Gormley **Through scale, *Field* makes the viewer feel big, and the expansion pieces make one feel rather small. Playing on scale (which is not the same as size) makes us feel our bodies-in-the-world.**

McGonagle How does that work with the concrete pieces?

Gormley **The block describes the space between the body and a compressed notion of architecture, and what I find makes them quite tender is that the principle gesture of all those works is touch. Materiality in sculpture invites touch. They don't. The body that touches is not there and what is touched is space, engaging the air. The concrete has become, as it were, a necessary conditionality. The work has always identified the minimum space necessary for a man to occupy but I think the concrete pieces do it in a more intimate, open and direct way. There is a real point of contact with the particularity of my body – slipped from life into art, with every wrinkle of the knuckles embedded in the concrete. Maybe the concrete works have found a new way of engaging with the central premises of Western sculpture: the relationship of idea to raw materials, image to block.**

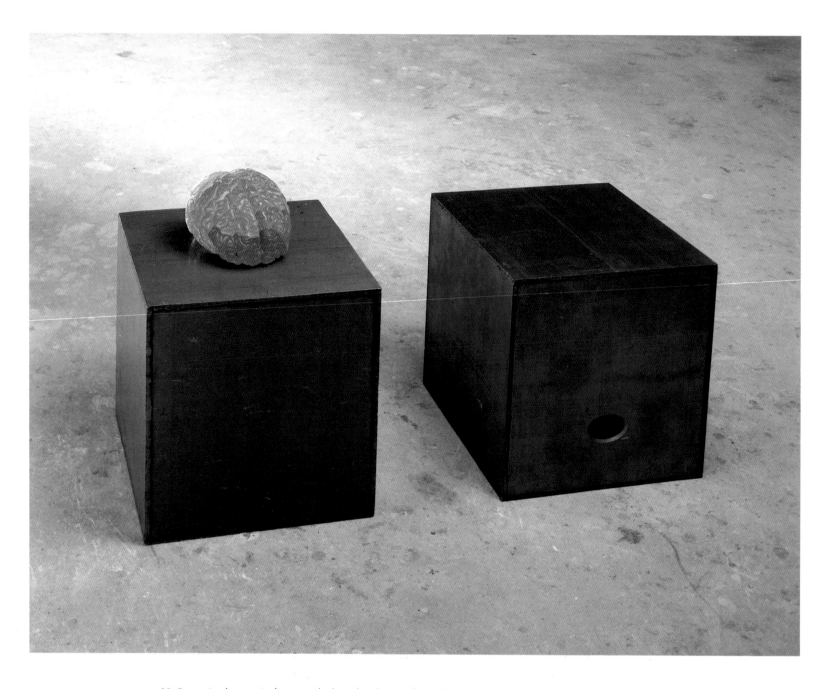

McGonagle Are you trying to articulate the silence of the Minimal cube?

Gormley **I think there are other kinds of silence, which are different from the silence of formal certainty, and which can encourage subjective response.**

McGonagle Judd has very powerfully mapped out an absolute in the physical and theoretical territory of his work. It's interesting that Jefferson mapped the Western states of the United States as a grid, as absolutes, and then sent the explorers Lewis and Clark to confirm them. Conception came before perception and demanded a complete invalidation of what and who was there originally and their relationship with the territory. Dominant forces simply do not recognize the 'other' and in that sense neither does puritanical Modernism.

Gormley **In *Field*, the earth is being allowed to carry the voice of the other to re-affirm the spirit of the land that lives through the people. The *American Field* has a strong presence of the original inhabitants of that continent. This is distinct from the pioneers' dreams of possession of the land, where a map is conceptualized ground. I want to make the ground fruitful for the mind. The grid you have drawn – that imposes on the**

Body and Light
1988/93
Lead, fibreglass, air, rosin
88 × 30.5 × 30.5 cm
Brain: 9 × 13 × 16 cm

Meaning
1988/93
Lead, fibreglass
30.5 × 30.5 × 30.5 cm

land – is distinct from the aboriginal intuition which is one of human consciousness being a continuation of the land, the feeling that they are embedded in the land, which is to do with the continuum between human and mineral life.

McGonagle There is a distinction here between the idea of living and the idea of being lived. Aboriginal cultures across the world have different concepts of possession of the land. Since there now seems to be a terminal sense to nineteenth century expansive Capitalism – of which Modernism is a product – different possibilities must exist for collaborative relationships, such as those involved in making a work like *Field*, in Mexico, and then the making and showing of it elsewhere, as you have done in Malmö, and will do in St. Helens.

Gormley **There are lots of things to talk about here, but for me, one of the most important things is that through sharing the engendering of the work, the makers are also the work's first audience and it is not like the audience of a spectacle. It's more like a collective experience of active imaginative involvement. I am inviting a group of people to spend some time with the earth in a way that they wouldn't normally do, to touch it again and again. There is a ritual which is important. We work on the floor at the level of the work.**

McGonagle Could you call it harvesting?

Gormley **It is a kind of harvesting – it's about tilling the earth with your hands but instead of making something grow, it is the earth you are forming directly. The harvest comes from within the people, or the thing that is growing comes out of the people. Everyone has their own row and throughout the project they continue to do row after row on the same strip like the old medieval strip field and they build up a very strong relationship with that patch of earth. Those gazes that they are seeding in the clay look back at them as they are working, suggesting that consciousness is not only inside. I see it as a kind of soul garden. It is a fragile thing but it is a link – both personal to the person who is making them and also common to all of us – something to do with the way in which the figures house the memory. That memory is transpersonal and yet we all have a personal relationship with the future. For me, *Field* is the consummation of being the other, a kind of liberation in many ways – of many ways.**

Antony Gormley (cat.), Konsthall Malmö, Sweden; Tate Gallery Liverpool; Irish Museum of Modern Art, Dublin, 1993

Allotment 1996

I propose to ask 300 local people – men, women and children of all ages – to co-operate with me in making a work. The participants will be asked to have themselves measured standing. The following measurements will be taken:

In front

1   The total height from the top of the head to the ground.
2   From the shoulder to the ground.
3   From the shoulder to the top of the head.
4   The width of the head.
5   The height of the top of the ear from the top of the head.
6   The length of the ear.
7   The height of the mouth from the division of the lips.
8   The width of the mouth.
9   From side to side at the widest.
10 The height of the anus from the floor.

In profile

11 From the back to the front at the deepest (i.e. from the buttocks to the toes).
12 The distance from the tip of the toes to the tip of the nose.
13 From the tip of the nose to the back of the head.
14 The distance from the back of the head to the back of the ear.
15 The distance from the side of the head to the side of the body.

These measurements should then be used to construct three hundred 5 centimetre thick rectangular concrete body cases, with integrated rectangular head cases and apertures at the mouth, ears, anus and genitals. The dimensions of the apertures will be taken from the ear and mouth measurements as will the placement. The anus and genital apertures will be proportional to the volume of the piece (1.2 square centimetres to a cubic metre). The outside of the ear apertures will be a square based on the length of the ear. The apertures will be angled to an internal opening of 6 square millimetres.

The anus and genital holes will be angled at 45 degrees. The mouth aperture will be square and based on the width of the mouth. The top of the ear holes will be at the position of the top of the ears. The mouth hole will be centred on the line of the lips. The anus and genital holes will be at the anus level on the internal wall of the case.

The pieces will be of poured concrete using standard wooden shuttering ply for both

left, opposite and overleaf,
Allotment II
1996
Hollow reinforced concrete
300 lifesize units from people
aged 1.5 to 80 years, dimensions
variable
Installation, Malmö Konsthall,
Sweden

the internal void and the external surface, with 5 millimetre galvanized steel reinforcing on a 10 centimetre grid. The pieces will be poured upside down, the head sections poured first, then the body section. The pieces will be cured over a ten day period. The concrete will be constituted from seven parts white cement and one part grey cement, four parts silver sand and eight parts 4 millimetre white quartz chippings.

Once made, the pieces will be placed in a large space: the Malmö Konsthall.

The composite work will evoke a surrogate cityscape with the pieces laid on a grid path system wide enough for a viewer to pass through. Some will be closely packed next to each other, some less so. They will face all directions. The viewer, having apprehended the work initially as a whole, will then be able to make his/her way through the composition engaging with pieces intimately.

Betong (cat.), Malmö Konsthall, Sweden, 1996.

Allotment: Interview with Hans Anderson 1996

Allotment I
1995
Solid reinforced concrete
112 lifesize units from people
aged 1.5 to 80 years, dimensions
variable
Installation, Herning
Kunstmuseum, Herning, Denmark

Hans Anderson Is *Allotment* site specific?

Antony Gormley **No, it can be shown anywhere, but it's important that the work results from an encounter with life: real lives registered through measurement, the intimacy of the body translated into the abstraction of numbers. But there is another side to it, connected with dreaming, in the sense that these are empty interiors which could accommodate the body but never will; thus they are void like ghosts, denied living bodies. The other aspect of this dream is the realization of a Modernist project, the making of a constructed landscape.**

    ***Allotment* has nothing to do with style but with trying to understand our situation. By doing things with scale – shrinking architecture to the skin – we can look again, as if we were aliens observing an environment and seeing it freshly, for the first time. *Allotment* can provoke reflection on how we fit into the world we have constructed.**

Anderson In contemporary cities, many people feel they are living in an environment over which they have no influence. Does this work have a political agenda?

Gormley **I'm not making a manifesto, there's no political slogan like 'at the end of the twentieth century we have outgrown the city and mankind should colonize the desert'. I'm trying to say 'here we are' and then ask what is 'here', and how are 'we'? Many of the adjectives used about contemporary art: boring, cold, distant, have a certain truth. There's no moral implication, this is an 'objective appraisal' of our condition. Maybe the first job that art has to do is to mirror life but it also has to act as a catalyst for concentrating it so that through art we are put in a position where we can change.**

    What you are saying is true, many people feel that they don't have a choice, they feel stuck. In the same way that we have inherited plumbing and sewerage systems from the last century so we inherit a way of life that keeps us stuck in a certain strata of possibilities, but art can provide an alternative realm. So I think that there is politics in the work, but it's not a political message that has found sculpture as its mouthpiece. *Allotment* opens the question of the monument and asks if we can make artworks that can become a reservoir of collective hope and fear like *Field*. Both works are intimate in scale but achieve their monumentality through an organic process: their size grows and has the potential of infinite extension. They re-negotiate scale in a way that is different from the huge single object, and they reverse the traditional monument's concern with memorial and the past. Both works are concerned with the future: with what will be.

What I like about rethinking the monumental is that it returns art to a natural, inevitable form that goes beyond something that can be owned.

   Allotment asks what happens to us when we accept the structures necessary to life in large groups. It replicates the social engineering that surrounds us. I pass a tower block in the same way that in the Australian outback I might pass a termite mound. I recognize a habitat that often I don't want to think about. It's the densest level of urban life but, for some, a forgotten strata. […] The piece isn't a diatribe against the evils of modern city life; one of the benefits of living close together is that the energy is very high, with high levels of contact. I wouldn't live anywhere else. I'm not saying we should all go and live in 'nature'; we can't: anywhere we go is transformed. In making this experiment I'm saying, 'This is where we come from; do we recognize it?'

   Le Corbusier and Mies van der Rohe realized that if we get the relationship between light and space right, living becomes its own decoration. That's a beautiful idea. What do we mean when we say we need room, and what is this need about?

Anderson Each of the many figures in *Allotment* is solitary, yet also related to the others.

Gormley **Have you ever lived in a commune?**

Anderson No, I haven't.

Gormley **I lived communally twice, a very practical way of living. What we're negotiating in the cities is the balance between the rights of each of us to self determination and the demands of communal living. The *sine qua non* of collective life is collective space, both physical and imaginative. We need to make public space because as we haven't valued it, it's been taken from us, destroyed by commercial interests and by the car. This piece asks where is collective space and how do we begin to articulate it?**

Anderson What you say is quite the opposite of what most sociologists say: that we are becoming more and more egotistical; that we don't care about anything collective; that we're just looking out for ourselves.

Gormley **An 'I, me, mine' culture. However we stand at the threshold of a virtual world which promises us a cyber-community. This means that the displacement of consciousness is well underway and that perhaps the greatest public spaces are non physical and**

Artist's Writings

Allotment I
1995
Solid reinforced concrete
112 lifesize units from people
aged 1.5 to 80 years, dimensions
variable
Installation, Hvide Sande,
Denmark

those of the electronic media: the Internet, interactive television, radio. Against this background I'm interested in asking questions about physical presence, and its correlative, physical space; asking questions about rootedness – what is our relationship with the earth and with its correlative, stellar and imaginative space? There must be a celebration of the body to balance the inevitable rise of the virtual world. I'm not actually frightened of the technology and there are great advantages in being able to communicate so widely and cheaply. But it should encourage us to reconnect with pre-linguistic experience. We are now so surrounded by mediated experience through the image, the written and the spoken word. The body is a ground on which a balance can be struck between the internal registration of direct experience – whether that's plunging into the sea or climbing a mountain, or making love to someone that you care very much about, all of which reinforces us – and linguistic or coded negotiation with the outside world. When we do this we make a projection or a construction like a bridge. The body is the ground in which these two activities relate. It's the most important territory at the moment. In *Allotment* the place of the body has been voided. I'm inviting the viewer to fill the empty spaces with his or her own bodily experiences.

Each of these rooms has a number on the back which has an analogical function connecting to the way that identity is translated in social administration. But it also has a private function so that anybody who is measured can find their room. This is important, because otherwise the whole thing is just a metaphor, which it isn't. You could say these are bunkers for the survival of 300 individuals were there to be an aerial bombardment, or they could be used immediately as meditation cells.

Previously unpublished interview, Malmö Konsthall, 1996. Revised 2000.

Under My Skin
1997
Cast iron, steel
195 × 48 × 30 cm
opposite, Detail

Everything erasable; rewind, fast-forward, delete, record, re-record, forget …
Our appearance belongs to others, we live in the darkness of the body – part of all darkness but felt. The skin, on which light falls and which it renders visible, is useless for definition – but perhaps all definition is provisional; a necessary charting in our journey through uncertainty.

How can we make the interior felt and cheat the illusion of appearance? The work started as a kind of testing of objects, sometimes insulating them, sometimes cutting them, but in either case trying to allow the time in them to become visible. Sculpture is a direct way of allowing mind to dwell in matter. It is a means of becoming aware of the connections between matter, space and time in a way that complements (but is completely different from) the connections that science has demonstrated. I firmly believe that we are part of a chain of being and that sculpture is a way of providing instruments in which our place within it can be tested, made manifest and perhaps transformed.

Where does the world begin? Of course we make it moment by moment and most intimately in what we call the self – but world and self cannot be separated – they are continuous. Where consciousness ends and the world begins is not so easy to define. We are, after all, borrowing our bodies from the earth and is it not likely that the earth knows more of us than we of it? Nothing is ever lost. They say that we could hear the words of Buddha in the deer park at Sarnath if only we had instruments sensitive enough, since the vibrations of sound waves continue to reverberate. Chaos theory has perhaps helped us to realize again the connectedness of things. My proposition is that we are part of a world constructed from the earth, in which everything is interchangeable. My hope is that the old formula of a 'subject who looks' at an object which is 'looked at' can be transmuted into us looking at ourselves. The place of my body is offered as yours and the space and actions of your body are reflected in the works, what they are made of and how they are made. Nothing is revealed that is not already there – including you.

First published as artist's statement in *Still Moving: Works 1975–1996* (cat.), Japan Association of Art Museums, Tokyo, 1996. Revised 2000.

Still Moving (extracts) 1996

What is the difference between our experience of time now and that of twenty-five years ago? I feel that today we are in a state of movement in spite of ourselves, and perhaps we are more aware now of being a subject who is moved, rather than an active participant who is moving […] The most profound and appropriate monument that we are bequeathing to the future is undoubtedly our network of motorways and roads that speak of restlessness. They are the creation of a time in which an ever greater taste for mobility has perhaps been the most constant feature of life.

Paul Virilio writes eloquently about this current condition of *déplacement*, and sees this mirrored in the way in which the place of inscription of art has itself become more and more mobile […] I want to ask whether it is possible for art to resist the flow of displacement by creating places – works that answer a need for shared experience that is not 'religious' in the conventional sense but invite those experiencing them to reflect on their own purpose.

Can we use the space of art for communion? A contact not only between ourselves but between ourselves and history? In doing this can we also derive the energy necessary to believe in our part in the construction of the future? Is it possible for art to provide a space that can be regenerative? Is it possible to use the space of art to resist this restlessness, this sense of fragmentation, this sense of alienation from self and from place?

My feeling is that in spite of our mobility and that of contemporary visual media, and perhaps because of these things, we still yearn to see within the built environment, within the agricultural environment that surrounds it and even in the less touched, natural environment, something that connects with our deepest fears and our most profound hopes. What has happened with collective expression exercised in collective space (particularly in Europe between 1903 and 1940 and in the former Soviet Union for much longer) is that the creative need expressed in the stone avenues and circles of megalithic cultures or in the gothic cathedrals of Europe has been subverted by totalitarian political use. I think that there is not a great distinction here between the legacy of hundreds of tons of bronze empress/goddesses from the Indian Raj and the monuments of Stalinism, National Socialism and Fascism. They all subverted a natural desire within humankind to make creative changes to their environment so that it could act as a witness to their lives, serving as an energizer, focus, resonator, extending the imaginative into the physical and vice-versa. This is the impulse behind the megalithic monuments and even the cathedrals: a collective endeavour, addressing sidereal time with an object that is also a location, made of stone or some enduring material; an

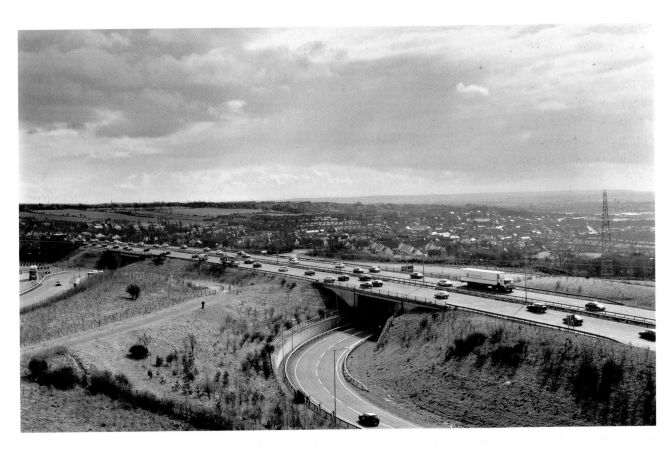

View of A1 road from the head of
Angel of the North
1998
Gateshead, Tyne and Wear

object that exists beyond the span of a human life. From this place (for it is important that it be a place as well as an object) we can project into the time to come.

It is more important to respond to this yearning now than at any other time. Virilio may be right that the technology of the virtual world of TV and the Internet is making the production and reception of the work of art practically synchronic and completely displaced. Yet I think there is a necessary resistance to this, which reinforces the primary experience in the body that the virtual world is constantly trying to leave behind. I don't want you to think that I am anything but excited by the implications of the Internet. The Internet, for better or worse, is an objectification of Teilhard de Chardin's idea of the communion of human mind – the noosphere, which is the third encirclement of the globe, the first being the biosphere and the second the atmosphere. With this possibility of instant communication, created by a non-space that is everywhere, the idea of place becomes very important. It can be reinforced by the continuation of a collective art that in some way places human being in a much wider context. I say collective art not because I am arguing for a community art project as it has come to be understood since the 1960s but one that comes from a collective will to make 'a landmark'. This should be seen as the fulfilment of the movement in the late 1960s and 1970s in which artists went 'out into the wilderness' to make works that were 'essential' and escape the commodification of the market.

In philosophical terms, I think what I'm proposing is to return to the rootedness of Heidegger in order to contravene the deconstructive principles of Baudrillard. In 'The Origin of the Work of Art' Heidegger describes the Classical Greek temple as a form of paradigm for the collective expression of a people in a place.

'A building, a Greek temple, portrays nothing. It simply stands there in the middle of the rock cleft valley. The building encloses the figure of the God and, in this concealment, lets it stand out into the holy precinct through the open portico. By means of the temple the God is present in the temple. This presence of the God is in itself the extension and the limitation of the precinct as a holy precinct. The temple and its precinct, however, do not fade away into the indefinite. It is the temple work that first fits together and at the same time gathers around itself the unity of those paths and relations in which birth and death, disaster and blessing, victory and disgrace, endurance and decline, acquire the shape of destiny for human beings.'

I am interested in reviving this idea of presence. Can we have presence without the God? Can we resurrect the monument without bringing the shadow of bad history? The idea of an image that is open enough to be interpreted widely, that has multiple and generative potential for meaning but is strong enough to be a focus. How do we construct such an image? In its being someone's can it become everyone's? It has seemed for quite a long time obvious to me that the body can represent at the present time what abstraction did at the beginning of the twentieth century. That is, the ground on which all the seeds of emancipated identity are to grow: the last frontier, the inner realm. (Space has been probed but what do we really *know* of the body's darkness.) The body, not as an object of idealization that should be forced to carry allegorical, symbolic or dramatic readings, but the body as a place. The body not as hero or as sexual object, but the body in some way as the collective subjective – the place where we all live. The place on which the pressures of society are inscribed and out of which expression, language, feeling, can come.

From an address to the 'Art and Spirituality' conference, Durham Cathedral, October 1996. Revised 2000.

Another Place: A Proposal for the Wattenmeer, Cuxhaven 1997

Another Place
1997
Cast iron
100 figures, 189 × 53 × 29 cm
each
Installation over 3 km², Cuxhaven,
Germany

To install 100 solid cast iron body forms along the coast to the west and south of the 'Kugelbake'. The work will occupy an area of 1.75 square kilometres with the pieces placed between 50 and 250 metres apart along the tideline and one kilometre out towards the horizon, to which they will all be facing. Depending on the fall of the land, the state of the tide, the weather conditions and the time of day the work will be more or less visible. The sculptures will be installed on a level plane attached to two metre vertical steel piles; the ones closest to the horizon will stand on the sand, those nearer the shore being progressively buried. At high water the sculptures that are completely visible when the tide is out will be standing up to their necks in water.

The sculptures are made from 17 body casts taken from my body (protected by a thin layer of wrapping plastic) between 19 May and 10 July 1997. The sculptures are all standing in a similar way, with the lungs more or less inflated and their postures carrying different degrees of tension or relaxation.

I was originally asked to show *Field* (40,000 hand–sized terracotta figures) in the spectacular 200 metre-long Hapag immigration halls that stretch to the sea on the Amerika Hafen. This got me thinking about distance and departure and to reflecting that when things get tough we think of somewhere else – somewhere that is not here and now: the birth of the New World. The physical journey that immigrants to the United States make is mirrored tragically in the recent Hale-Bopp cult's mass exodus and more domestically in the journeys that all of us make when we go on holiday; we all dream of the Promised Land.

Thus the epic is made domestic. This is also apparent in our attempts to make the seaside into a living room, replete with notices, furniture, bathrooms, etc., framing the terrors of the ocean with comfort and ignoring the lure of the horizon. Into this context of tame sublimity I have introduced 100 cloned foreign bodies, so far spaced that when the beach is crowded they will, to the unaware eye, be invisible, but at dawn and dusk the Wattenmeer will be theirs.

In placing art at the sea's edge I am asking about our relationship with nature, or our nature in nature, and the seaside is a good place to do this. Here time is tested by tide, architecture by the elements, and the prevalence of sky seems to question the earth's substance. In this work human life is tested against planetary time. A return of feeling in art cannot be accomplished without the body, however the body in art cannot simply return to its old haunts – the plinth, the museum – nor any of its old support structures. It has to be exposed and reconsidered by its infiltration within the world that we have made of this earth. This sculpture exposes to light and time the nakedness of a particular and peculiar body; no hero, no ideal, just the industrially reproduced body of a middle-aged man trying to remain standing and trying to breathe, facing a horizon busy with ships moving blocks of coloured containers around the planet.

First published in *Gormley/Theweleit*, Schleswig-Holsteinischer Kunstverein; Cuxhaven Kunstverein, Germany, 1999.

Insiders 1999

What is an Insider? An Insider is to the body what memory is to consciousness: a kind of residue, something that is left behind. It is a core rather than a skeleton. It is a way of allowing things that are internal to the body – attitudes and emotions embedded in posture or hidden by gesture – to become revealed. They are equally alien and intimate.

The idea is that the pieces carry in concentrated form the trace of the body and its passage through life. This has a direct relationship to pain. I see these reduced forms as antennae for a particular kind of resilience that exists within all of us, that allows us to bear suffering but is itself created through painful experience. There is no judgement about this. Their bareness is not the nakedness that reveals the flesh; it is the result of having had the flesh taken away, a loss which is not sentimentalized but accepted. The Insider tries to up the ante between being and nothingness.

I want them to endure in time and concentrate space. They are made in a durable and relatively permanent base element: iron. The earth has iron at its core and these are like the cooled and revealed magnetic load cores of the body.

Insiders started as an experiment, a reduction or concentration of the body which was a reverse procedure from the expansion of the body that had concerned me in the late 1980s and early 1990s. It resulted initially from the reduction of the body that was necessary in the production of the *Angel of the North*, where the body form had to be reduced all over by 12.5 metres in order for the 20 radial ribs to exist half within and half without the original body skin.

The first work that dealt with the Insider theme was *Under My Skin* (1997) in which a relatively relaxed body form was reduced all over by 12.5 mm and this surface replaced by the ends of over 3,000 pins (each 12.5 mm long) that were nailed into the surface. This work led me on to experiment with proportional reduction and, after a number of attempts, to *Insider I*, a work in which all the limbs were taken separately and reduced by sixty per cent on a longitudinal axis, leaving the body the same height but diminishing its cross-section.

The series continued, from *Insider II* to *XIV,* and occupied me from 1996 to 1999. They are all two-thirds reductions of my body, apart from the last four, in which I used the bodies of three women who were strange to me, and a work based on my first child when just able to stand.

The reductions are achieved by hand, through cutting around 130 cross-sections through the body mould, reducing all of them through measurement and then replacing the reduced cross-sections with the mould and welding them together so that they keep their place precisely at the centre of the form. The only designed parts are the

Installation, 'Trialogo: Giuseppe
Gallo, Antony Gormley, David
Hammons', Palazzo delle
Esposizioni, Rome, 2000
foreground, **Insider III**
1998
Cast iron
244 × 40 × 27 cm

middle, **Insider IV**
1998
Cast iron
193 × 55 × 27 cm

back, **Insider II**
1997
Cast iron
193 × 191 × 27 cm

left and overleaf, left, **Insider IX**
1998
Work in progress, the artist's
studio

overleaf, right, **Insider VII**
1998
Cast iron
192 × 54.5 × 28 cm

Insider VIII
1998
Cast iron
184.5 × 56 × 38 cm

Insider V
1998
Cast iron
194.5 × 49.5 × 47 cm

Insider IX
1998
Cast iron
174.5 × 49.5 × 47 cm

bridges between the torso and limbs at the hips and shoulders, and between the chest and the breasts or the hips and the penis.

This process of objective mathematical reduction leads to a particular form of abstraction, a found object never revealed before and certainly not invented. It's a body that lies within all of us. In the exhibition 'Intimate Relations' (Jablonka Galerie, Cologne, 1999, the three female forms test the universality of the Insider across sex and the body of the 'other' and are joined by the Insider of a baby boy at that stage in his development when he is just able to stand. He looks up to us to be recognized in an arena constituted by the archetypes of mother, sister and lover.

The Insider suggests also that the most intimate is the most strange, that inside each of us is a self that we would maybe rather not recognize, and which constitutes a kind of third man, the Insider as alien witness.

Trialogo: Giuseppe Gallo, Antony Gormley, David Hammons (cat.), Palazzo delle Esposizioni, Rome, 2000.

Contents

'*The continuation into the twentieth century of a traditional treatment of the human figure is not given a place in these pages …*'
　– Rosalind Krauss, *Passages in Modern Sculpture* (1977)

'*Sculpture: the embodiment of the truth of Being in its work of instituting places.*'
– Martin Heidegger, 'Art and Space' (1969)

'*It is undeniable that from man, as from a perfect model, statues and pieces of sculpture … were first derived.*'
　– Giorgio Vasari, *Lives of the Artists* (1568)

Sculpture is the most ancient, conservative and intractable of the media. 'The material in which God worked to fashion the first man was a lump of clay', notes Vasari,[1] and the result was a notoriously rebellious sculptural self-portrait, since God took himself as the model and formed Adam (or Adam and Eve together) 'in his image'. You know the rest of the story. God breathes life into the clay figures. They have minds of their own, rebel against their creator, and are punished for it by being condemned to leave their paradisal home and work all their lives, only to die and return to the shapeless matter from which they emerged. Variations of this myth appear in many cultures and materials: Prometheus' creation of man from clay; the Jewish Golem; the clay statuettes animated by the Great Spirit in Hopi legend; Pygmalion falling in love with his own statue; 'the modern Prometheus', Dr Frankenstein, who uses dead bodies as material for his rebellious creatures; the

metallic humanoids of contemporary science fiction, the 'post-human' creatures known as robots and cyborgs.

There is a circular process at work in these narratives. Man is both the sculpted object and the sculpting agent, both created as and creator of sculpted images. God introduces man and other creatures into the world by means of the art of sculpture. Then man brings sculpture (and gods) into the world by creating material images of himself and other creatures. The dangerous moment is invariably associated with animation, when the sculpted object takes on 'a life of its own' – when it begins to speak, move, breathe, acquire consciousness, act on its own or (most simply) when people begin to believe that the sculpted object can do these things, and to project life into them. The god of monotheism, the deity of Judaism, Christianity and Islam, understands that image-making as such is a dangerous business and establishes an absolute prohibition on it:

'*Thou shalt not make unto thee any graven image, or any likeness of any thing that is in heaven above, or that is in the earth beneath, or that is in the water under the earth*:

'*Thou shalt not bow down thyself to them, nor serve them: for I the Lord thy God am a jealous God, visiting the iniquity of the fathers upon the children unto the third and fourth generations of them that hate me.*'[2]

Vasari understood that this prohibition spelled trouble for the arts, and especially the art of sculpture. So he resorts to a familiar distinction: '*It was the worship given to statues, not the making of them, which was wickedly sinful*'.[3] Vasari then

Havmann
1994-95
Granite
10.1 × 3.3 × 2.2 m
Permanent installation, Mo-i-Rana, Norway
above, Inauguration

cites the usual precedents: '*The art of design and of sculpture, in all kinds of metal as well as marble, was taught by God … They made the two golden cherubim, the candlesticks and the veil, and the hems of the sacerdotal vestments, all the beautiful casts for the Tabernacle*.'[4] Vasari finesses the question of images of the human form and ignores (as he must) the clear language of the Second Commandment, which prohibits 'the making' of statues as such, not just the worship of them.

The Second Commandment seems to presume a 'slippery slope' principle of image-making: if one allows human beings to make statues or images of any kind, the images will sooner or later take on a life of their own and ultimately become objects of worship. Better to stop the whole process at its origin or insist on arts that refuse all image-making, figuration or representation, arts of pure ornamentation or abstraction. Sculpture, especially the kind modelled on the human body, is not only the first but the most dangerous of the arts. It impiously elevates the human image to the status of a god, reifies mortal men into immortal idols and degrades spirit into dead matter.

Sometimes it seems, then, as if sculpture achieves its truest vocation not when it is erected but when it is pulled down. Adam has not only feet of clay but an entire body made of fragile, biodegradable material; he is built to fall. Statues, as Antony Gormley has observed (and demonstrated in his recent work) may take on more force if they look abandoned or 'deposed': 'even a deposed statue has meaning, potency, and relevance.'[5] Indeed, Shelley's 'Ozymandias' suggests that monumental sculpture finds its truest vocation

when the statue is in ruins, and its boastful inscription 'Look on my works, ye Mighty and despair' takes on a new meaning, precisely the opposite of the original intention.

Let us fast forward now to the present day, when these archaic and mythical taboos on sculpture seem at best a faint and distant memory. What place does sculpture have in the contemporary system of the arts? Has it been swallowed up, along with photography, painting, collage and technical media into an overarching art of spectacle, of display, installation and environmental design, a media-scape of infinitely malleable and de-materialized images? Or does it have a distinctive role to play as a specific medium linked with its immeasurably long and deep history? What role, more specifically, does sculpture oriented towards the human body have to play in our time?

Certainly sculpture played a key role in the unfolding of artistic Modernism and Postmodernism. Every abstract movement in modern painting had its sculptural counterpart. Minimalist sculpture and the readymade even dared to challenge painting in its quest for supremacy in the negation of figuration and representation. Sculpture in the 1960s expressed concerns, as the artist Robert Morris put it, 'not only distinct but hostile to those of painting'.[6] Paintings, as critic Michael Fried lamented, began to take on 'object-hood',[7] asserting their three-dimensional physical presence in real space, or becoming themselves something like cabinets for the storage of more objects of three-dimensional manipulation.

But sculpture, whether it obeyed Fried's Modernist imperative (exemplified by David Smith and Anthony Caro) of virtuality, opticality, gestural significance and anti-theatrical autonomy, or asserted itself in what art critic Rosalind Krauss called its 'expanded field', has still seemed to many a kind of homeless art. Does it belong in a sculpture garden? A special wing of the museum? Next to an architectural monument like the parsley garnish next to a roast? An ornament to the public plaza, as an invisible prop like the typical work of 'public art'? An obtrusive barrier like Richard Serra's *Tilted Arc* (1981)? Or off in the wilderness, a disappeared monument, like Robert Smithson's *Spiral Jetty* (1970)?

The question of place, site or location has always been a central issue for sculpture. Unlike painting, it normally does not carry its frame with it, and is thus much more sensitive to issues of placement. It does not project a virtual space, opening a window into immensity as (say) land-scape painting does; it *takes up* space, moves in and occupies a site, obtruding on it or changing it. It risks failure on two fronts, by being too obtrusive (Serra) or too passive (the statue as perch for pigeons). There seems to be an ideal middle place, a Utopia for sculpture, hinted at in the notion of the 'genius loci', the spirit of place embodied in the sculptural figure that seems to belong to a place, to express its inner being, and to 'activate' the place by incarnating its special character.[8]

But this notion of sculpture as rooted in a specific place, organically connected with its site, seems like an archaic and nostalgic residue, perhaps appropriate for a primitive, sedentary society, deeply connected to the land. It reeks of Heideggerean mysticism, of clearings in the wilderness, 'the release of places at which a god appears',[9] as when the dryad or tree spirit is 'released' from its prison by the sculptor who carves a figure from the trunk. What possible application could it have for modern cultures caught up in vortices of mobility, flow and instantaneous global communication? What is the place of sculpture – especially sculpture focused on the human body – today?

Antony Gormley's sculpture constitutes a profound reflection on sculpture and place, understood in the broadest possible sense. 'Place' includes both physical and institutional sites, the cultural location of sculpture among the arts and media as well as its placement in real space. It also designates the sculptural work itself as a place or space, a specific site that occupies or 'displaces' a certain volume, opening a hollow or body-scape, an interior more or less distinguish-able from an exterior. As Heidegger puts it, 'things themselves are places and do not merely belong to a place.'[10] This is especially true when the *thing* is a human body or a sculptural representation of it. The human body is the most highly charged place in our experience. It is an inescapable prison and the portal to every conceivable flight of fantasy.

Gormley's work comes at the problem of space by raising the question of 'what sculpture wants' – that is, both what it desires or longs for, and what it *lacks* – in our time, and (as is argued later) in any time whatsoever. What sculpture wants is a place to stand, a site, a location both literally and figura-tively, and Gormley's work provides a profound expression of this longing for space. Like the naked human body which is the first model for and object

above, left, **Richard Serra**
Tilted Arc
1981
Cor-Ten steel
$366 \times 3,658 \times 16.5$ cm
Installed, Federal Office Plaza,
New York. Later removed

above, right, **Robert Smithson**
Spiral Jetty
1970
Rock, salt crystals, earth, water
ø approx. 457 m
Great Salt Lake, Utah

Stand
1997
Cast iron
9 figures, 196 × 48 × 35 cm each
Installation, Hanaskog, Sweden

of sculpture, it is both a homeless wanderer, an exile from the Edenic Utopia where it was the genius of the place, and itself the home that it can never completely abandon. Sculpture wants both a place to be, and to be a place.

These remarks initially appear to be out of step with contemporary thinking about the arts on at least two fronts. First, the attribution of desires to a medium and the specific images that appear within it, seems like a flirtation with animism or totemism, the personification of inanimate objects and the entire set of practices (the medium) in which those objects are produced.[11] Second, the suggestion that there is a transcendental or at least abiding set of problems associated with the medium of sculpture, seems like a lapse into ahistorical formalism. However, it is only by risking an exploration of the deeply abiding conditions of an artistic medium that we can hope to specify its historical modulations with any precision.[12] Only by exploring the human attribution of agency, aura, personhood and animacy to artificial objects can we hope to understand those objects, the media in which they appear, and the effects they have on beholders.

Statues: Sculpture as Place

'*Statue n. L. statua, f. sta-, root of* stare *to stand ... 1. A representation in the round of a living being, sculptured, moulded, or cast in marble, metal, plaster or the like materials; esp. a figure of a deity, allegorical personage, or eminent person, usually of life-size proportions. Also transf. and* similitave, *as a type of silence or absence of movement or feeling.*'
– Oxford English Dictionary

Gormley's importance begins with his insistence on taking the human body – specifically his own body – as his principal subject matter. This may seem so obvious as to require no notice. But it is, from the standpoint of advanced, sophisticated thinking in the art world at the threshold of the twenty-first century, something like a polemical gesture. For an entire century, the most important sculpture has been more or less abstract, rendering the human body as an object to be deformed, extruded, deconstructed, fragmented or mutilated. There is no 'human' body anymore: there is the gendered body, the desiring body, the racialized body, the medical body, the sculpted body, the techno-body, the body in pain or pleasure. The human body has come to seem like an infinitely malleable assem-blage of prostheses and spare parts, an expression of a 'post-human' sensibility and a 'cyborg' consciousness.[13] The ideal form of the integral body – especially of the white, male body – as expressed in all those familiar diagrams of Renaissance and Romantic humanism – has seemed like an archaism or an exploded ideology to be surpassed or, even worse, a reminder of patriarchal idols and fascist monumentalism that we can do without. A casual encounter with Gormley's work, especially with the castings of his own body for which he is best known, is likely to lead to a snap judgment that his project is retrograde, redundant, a step backward into figurative sculpture and an out-moded humanism, masculinism and egotism.[14] An early admirer 'didn't dare tell anybody' how much he liked Gormley's statues because he 'thought they were very unfashionable'. And indeed they were and are. How dare a contemporary sculptor, in full knowledge of a century's sculptural experimentation which from Constructivism to Minimalism has renounced the 'statue', simply return to the human body, much less *his own* body, as subject, model and content of his art? Antony Gormley has taken this dare. The results are worth looking at and thinking about.

The first dare is the risk of what cultural theorist Judith Butler calls 'gender trouble'.[15] How can we 'place' the sexual identity of Gormley's statues? Gormley makes castings of his own unambiguously male body. They are sites of male identification, with phallic marks sometimes accentuated. Gormley also has the good (or bad) fortune to possess a rather beautiful, 'sculpturesque' body that inevitably reminds a beholder of the male body as the archaic figure of the idealized, normative human form – the very image that allows us to say 'man' or 'mankind' when we mean 'human'. The primal scene of sculpture in Genesis reinforces this sort of association, the creation of 'man' as the original creative act of the divine artist, the creation of woman as a kind of surgical dismemberment of the male body. The female body is not, in the first instance, sculpted but encased inside the male, to be delivered from the male 'womb' by a kind of Caesarean section. Adam is the first sculptural production, Eve the first reproduction. In Judaeo-Christian myth, man is made, woman is born.

Gormley's work complicates these stereotypes by activating the distinction between sex and gender at both the level of visual appearance and in the productive processes that 'engender' the sculpted object. It is a standard doctrine of

feminist theory, notes Judith Butler, that '*whatever biological intractability sex appears to have, gender is culturally constructed*'.[16] 'Man *and* masculine *might just as easily signify a female body as a male one, and* woman *and* feminine *a male body as easily as a female one*'.[17] If Gormley's sculpted figures are 'intractably' coded as biologi-cally male, their postures evoke the 'feminine' codes of passivity, vulnerability, abjection and receptivity. One might say that Gormley has a male body but uses it to express 'feminine' (even perhaps feminist) attitudes. Or that his figures express mixed messages about the relation of sex and gender, the 'intractable' facts of the material, biological body and its 'constructed' cultural form. More fundamentally, his work seems to deconstruct (while evoking) the differences between sex and gender, nature and culture. How, after all, do we know that the penis 'belongs to' the male of the species? Is its possession necessary or sufficient for 'manhood' or masculinity? As Butler argues, '*Gender is not to culture as sex is to nature; gender is also the discursive/cultural means by which "sexed nature" or "a natural sex" is produced and established as "prediscursive"*'.[18] Gormley makes visible the way the murmur of discourse is woven into the natural materiality of the human body and its sculptural traces. Once this dialectic of sex and gender has been unleashed, as it is in Gormley's body sculptures, it is not so easily stabilized.

An even more fundamental issue is the distinction between the gendering and *engendering* of human bodies. Real human bodies are both gendered and engendered. They are marked and re-marked by sexual difference and gender identity,

top, **Leonardo da Vinci**
Rule for the Proportions of the
Human Figure, According to
Vitruvius
Ink on paper
34.5 × 24.5 cm

above, **William Blake**
Urizen
1794
Colour-printed relief etching, ink,
watercolour
26 × 18 cm

but they are produced and reproduced by the interplay of bodies, even by a kind of autopoesis in the case of cloning or parthenogenesis. What about the engendering of sculpture, the processes of its production and reproduction?

There are two traditional ways[19] of making sculpture: carving or moulding from the outside (as in the creation of Adam), and casting from inside out (as in the birth of Eve).[20] Gormley's 'corpographs' work in the second mode. He casts himself in a full-body life mask of plaster; the resulting 'negative' is then used to cast a positive image in molten metal. The shaping tool is not the hand but the artist's entire body, and it works from within matter, holding open a space within it rather than sculpting away material from outside.

Like the Minimalist objects which are among their sculptural ancestors, they refuse all gesture or narrative syntax, forcing the spectator's attention back onto a specific object, this body, understood as a place, a space where someone has lived.[21] This procedure is so simple and obvious that it seems a wonder that no one had ever quite thought of doing it before. Casting the whole body as a life (or death) mask, the self-portrait, the monumentalizing of the human form in the static, standing figure – literally, the statue – all these resources had been available to sculpture, but never combined in quite this way. Why not? Perhaps because the results are visually subtle, even misleading: the casual observer may not know that these are casts of the artist's body and take them simply as generic figurative representations that seem 'old-fashioned' in their archaism and simplicity. Perhaps also because sophisticated

viewers dismiss the product for presenting the 'wrong look', no matter how original the process might be. This may be why Gormley often seems to be in the position of denying what seems like a self-evident appearance of his work. He claims that he was never really interested in figurative sculpture *per se* or even in 'representation' or copying more generally. However, his work does seem thoroughly mimetic and representational, not of the human body as a narrative agent or actor, but as a purely contemplative figure, witnessing and enduring in poses of suspended animation. Gormley subjects the processes of sculptural representation to a critique and re-shaping, so that the apparently familiar, recognizable results (lifesize anthropomorphic statues, most notably) radiate a strange sense of inward animation and sentient presence that is the abiding goal of (and phobia about) sculpture. Gormley's figurative statues are 'uncanny' in Freud's sense of the word. That is, they are not visibly weird or grotesque, but 'strangely familiar', both masculine and feminine, *heimlich* and *unheimlich*, homely and homeless.

A form of systematic doubleness, a perceptual 'double take', accompanies the experience of Gormley's statues. They are what Walter Benjamin called 'dialectical images', deeply ambiguous figures that fuse contrary forms of affect and interpretation, risking misapprehension so thoroughly that even the artist may seem 'in denial' of what is most manifest and obvious about them.

But Gormley is quite aware that his own work is no mere communication of messages he might want to send. He stresses, in fact, that the process

involves a necessary descent into blindness and unknowing.[22] Unlike a sculptor who steps back and looks at his work from outside as he carves it from stone, Gormley immerses himself in the material, encases himself, buries himself alive. He only sees what he has produced after the fact, at which point he has the option of going on with it, casting it further, or casting it aside.

What Gormley shows us, then, is that the body is a place, and that sculpture reveals (or hides) the shape of that place, the invisible interior space where someone lives or has lived. That place may be represented as a positive form, a 'statue' that has to be seen as a kind of embodied darkness (hence, perhaps, the frequent use of lead as material). The minimal form of this inner space is rendered in the *Insiders* series (1996-99), which tries to objectify the internal 'core' of the body by a process of subtraction and paring away, like the paring away of the outer rings of a tree to expose an earlier stage of its development. The obverse of this strategy can be seen in pieces such as *Rhizome I, II and III* (1998-99) in which the body's contours are augmented by some determinate quantity, and rendered as a biomorphic casing or 'pod' in which the basic shape of the hidden body has almost become imperceptible. The place of the body has also been indicated as an absence, a negative impression or void, as in *Bed* (1981), or the implied interior of an architectural or biomorphic 'case', as in *Flesh* (1990), *Sense* (1991) and *Fruit* (1991-93).

In these latter cases, the sculptural object may remind us of a tomb or a womb, a casket or a seed-pod in which the body is gestating. In the series

entitled *Allotment* (1997), the exterior is rendered in flat, horizontal surfaces of polished concrete, the only indication of the interior bodily shape being the orifices or holes where bodily appendages (feet, hands) might stick out, or the cubic 'capstones' that indicate the relation of head to body. These pieces, which an American viewer can hardly resist associating with the 'cement overshoes' (or overcoats) of mob executions, are at first glance among the most claustrophobic and chilling of Gormley's inventions. One imagines immediately what it would mean to inhabit the interior spaces of these concrete blocks, to be buried alive in stone. And yet the reference to modern architecture, reinforced when these works are assembled in miniature 'cities' renders them strangely familiar, even homely. It is as if we were suddenly allowed to see the modern apartment house, not as a box full of boxes, but as a box in which a single, unique human form has left its imprint throughout the structure. The effect is like a haunted Modernist high-rise, revealing the ghost within Le Corbusier's 'machine for living'.

opposite, **Rhizome III**
1999
Cast iron
425 × 260 × 306 cm
Installation, Lange Voorhout, The Hague, The Netherlands

above, left, **Rhizome I**
1998
Cast iron
310 × 80 × 315 cm
Installation, Umea, Sweden

above, right, **Rhizome II**
1998
Cast iron
498 × 380 × 340 cm
Installation, Parque Expo '98, Lisbon

This 'ghost' or empty space is both the imprint of a specific individual whose body provided the internal shape, and an evocation of the collective body of all the individuals that might inhabit the multiple spaces of such a building over time.

In all these cases (and 'case' here denotes both a physical container and an exemplary instance or problem for study) there is the sense of an impassive, almost featureless exterior hiding an explosive interior, much like the structure of a bomb. The *Insiders* are, as it were, the fuse or 'core' of the charged object; works such as the *Rhizome* series foreground the casing as biomorphic pod; in the *Allotment* series, the case is altered to refer to modern architecture. As Gormley has noted, 'The perfect form of sculpture is a bomb', a sentiment which again links his projects to the programme of Minimalism, recalling Robert Morris' unrealized *Bomb Sculpture*, and his treatment of the 'case' as a general sculptural problem.[23]

Inert or explosive objects, dead or living things, industrial relics or palaeontological fossils, individual or generic bodies, gendered or engendered identities, persons or places, archaic or contemporary works of art: the strange power of Gormley's 'statues' resides in the irresolvable tensions they activate among these alternative ways of 'seeing as'. They evoke the immemorial desire of sculpture to come alive as an animated image while resisting all the techniques (gesture, action, motion) that might give literal expression to this desire. Art theorist Stephen Bann puts this in terms relevant to the Second Commandment when he notes that 'Gormley's

works ... refuse to be idols in the same measure as they assert their right to be vehicles of presence.'[24]

But this is still only half (at most) of the story. Sculpture wants to be a place, wants to offer us a space for thought and feeling. It provides this place out of its own lack, its abject status or 'place' in the hierarchy of the arts as the medium of brute materiality – iron, lead, cement, mud – or (conversely) in its impression of serene detachment in a meditative, unconscious space beyond desire. But sculpture also wants a place to be, a location where it can be seen, encountered by other bodies. At this point all the dialectics of inner and outer form that have been activated in the shaping of a sculptural object are redoubled in the act of its placement in a setting or landscape. The statue has to find a place to stand. This longing for a place is as crucial to what sculpture wants as the desire that haunts the object itself.

Sites: Place as Sculpture

I placed a jar in Tennessee
And round it was, upon a hill.
It made the slovenly wilderness
Surround that hill.

The wilderness rose up to it,
And sprawled around, no longer wild.
The jar was round upon the ground
And tall and of a port in air.

It took dominion everywhere.
The jar was grey and bare.

It did not give of bird or bush,
Like nothing else in Tennessee.

– Wallace Stevens, 'Anecdote of the Jar'

If Gormley's sculpted objects are best seen as sites, they are also what Robert Smithson called 'non-sites' or displaced places. Like many artists of the 1960s, Smithson sought a way of moving out of the space of the gallery into other places – the 'wilderness' of the American West, the post-industrial wastelands of New Jersey. He brought back from these places material samples, geological maps and photographic documentation which reconstituted the gallery or space of exhibition as a non-site, a place defined by its reference to another place. Gormley does something similar, only in reverse. His mechanically reproduced 'corpographs' are already non-sites in themselves, like three-dimensional photographs that refer to the absent space of a body. These non-sites are then transported to a wide variety of places, some in traditional locations for sculpture (plazas, squares, museums, galleries) others in natural settings, most notably the magnificent blankness and expansiveness of the Australian desert and the tidal mud flats of Cuxhaven, Germany.

Wallace Stevens gives us a sense of the impact of a singular artifact upon a place. The lone figure, especially one stationed as a kind of witness or monitory presence, changes the whole sense of a place. As Heidegger suggests, the sculpted object 'institutes' the place as a human location, a site of gathering, rather than a mere location.

For Stevens, the eloquence and power of the figure is inversely proportional to its dramatic or gestural insistence. It is as if the more passive, non-committal and self-absorbed the figure, the more 'dominion' it exerts over the space around it.[25] Another way to see this is to ponder the scale of the human figure against the vastness of space. *Another Place* (1997), which places Gormley's figures on the tidal flats of Cuxhaven, clearly evokes the pictorial precedent of Caspar David Friedrich's painting *Monk by the Sea* (1809–10). The tiny figure of the monk against the vastness of the beach, sea and sky may seem at first to declare the insignificance of the figure. But a blink of the eye (or a moment's thought) reverses this impression, turning the landscape into what Gaston Bachelard called an 'intimate immensity'.[26] The landscape becomes an inscape, an interior space all the more evocative for its blankness.[27]

Another Place is notable, moreover, for the way it complicates the Romantic image of the lone, singular figure contemplating the vast, sublime landscape. In this work, Gormley multiplies the figures (as many as a dozen of them may be seen in a single panoramic photograph), dispersing them at intervals of several hundred yards, all facing out to sea. The effect is of a kind of stately procession into oblivion, as if a platoon of sentinels were pausing on their death march for a final look. The advancing and receding tide must enhance this sense that, as the sea rises and falls, the figures are descending into or emerging from the sea. Figure and ground each 'give away' their motion and stillness to the other.

overleaf, **Another Place**
1997
Cast iron
100 figures, 189 × 53 × 29 cm
each
Installation, Stavanger, Norway

Critical Mass (details)
1995
Cast iron
60 figures, lifesize
Installation, Royal Academy of
Art, London, 1998

So while the image of the sculpted figure that, like Stephens' jar or Friedrich's monk, 'takes dominion everywhere', dominating and organizing the wilderness, is evoked by Gormley's emplacements, it is not quite what they are after. The effect is more dialectical and interactive, a kind of mutual dislocation. This is most evident, perhaps, in Gormley's gallery installations, which sometimes recall Robert Morris' technique of re-orienting identical minimal objects in a variety of positions within the exhibition space, so that the form of a horizontal 'slab' would become equally a vertical monolith or a 'cloud' suspended from the ceiling.

Although Gormley's work has always been highly sensitive to issues of placement, his site installations in the last decade have been increasingly concerned with addressing the problem of the isolated and monumentalized singular figure. This concern is expressed in several ways: by a multiplication of figures; by an increasing tendency to breach the boundaries of the integral body; by an enhancement of the sense of 'alienness' and homelessness surrounding the figures, an expression of longing for place that remains rigorously and on principle unsatisfied by any particular location. An installation like *Critical Mass*, for instance, means one thing in a tram shed in Vienna (Stadtraum Remise, 1995), quite another in the courtyard of the Royal Academy in London (1998). In the Viennese setting, the combination of scattered, half-interred, suspended and witnessing bodies could evoke memories of the Holocaust among other associations. In London, the figures undercut the monumentality and heroism of the Western art traditions linked with the Academy. 'They're body forms without a place', Gormley notes,[28] that have been deliberately strewn and sewn like random seeds, eliciting the participation of a viewer who senses their incompleteness, latency and displacement. This last effect is perhaps most noticeable in the 'street' installations entitled *Total Strangers* (1996) that place figures both inside the traditional aesthetic space of the gallery and in the street, stationed as if they were homeless vagrants peering into shop windows or drunks sleeping off the night's excess in the lee of a building.

Photographs of interactions by passers-by with these figures are most telling. They suggest an intimacy and familiarity coupled with strangeness and dislocation. In contrast to the assertively central placement of typical public monuments (which are, as a consequence, usually ignored) Gormley's 'marginal' placements of figures where we would least expect them have the effect of producing a double-take, not unlike the shock one might feel on encountering George Segal figures in a park, or a hyper-realist figure by John De Andrea. The difference is that Segal depends on gestures of action, and De Andrea on a kind of *trompe-l'oeil* effect, a literal shock at taking something as alive that turns out to be a simulacrum. With Gormley, there is no simulation of the visual appearance of life. The works assert their status as statues, affirming the muteness and stillness of sculpture. If his figures 'simulate' anything like life, it is a transitional zone of sentience between consciousness and unconsciousness.

Gormley's most dramatic departure from the focus on his own figure isolated in a space

has been the series of works known as *Field* (1991–95), which evokes a whole range of precedents in Minimalist sculpture, recalling a variety of earthworks and non-sites, especially Walter de Maria's 'earth rooms' of the mid 1970s, and the emphasis on seriality, the body and space. It has been read as a host of lost (or saved?) souls assembling for the last judgment, as the incarnate spirits of unborn foetuses yearning for incarnation, as the resurrected victims of the Holocaust demanding justice, as a parable of the specific sites from which these figures emerge as a kind of local 'earthwork', or as a global allegory of displacement and diaspora, as if the 'huddled masses' of immigrants, exiles, homeless and refugees were all assembled in a single space. Each of these interpretive frameworks casts the spectator in a different role as well, inviting us to bask in the glow of mass attention or recoil from the sense of accusation and impossible demand. The 'double takes' elicited by Gormley's singular figures are vastly multiplied with this work and have an effect (which Winckelmann observed in the highest achievements of Classical sculpture) of fascination and astonishment – quite literally, a momentary turning of the spectator into something like a statue, stunned into contemplative stillness.

The notion of 'collective representation', the condensation of a social totality into a single gestalt, is central to what the anthropologist Emile Durkheim called 'totemism'.[29] Totems occupy a 'middle' place in the realm of sacred objects: unlike idols they are generally not images of gods but of sacred animals or plants; unlike fetishes, they are not associated with body parts, obsession or magical ritual but are integral forms linked with the identity of a community or tribe. The totem is literally (in its origin in the Ojibway language) 'a relative of mine', a figure that mediates social difference (exogamous sexual relations, tribal distinctions) with a sense of social solidarity and collective identity. (William Blake's figure of the giant Albion, who contains the whole universe in his body, is an important English precedent.) Gormley's rendering of the 'body of the multitude' (a 'host' in another sense) is another of his forays into the most archaic sculptural traditions.[30] This figure receives its most ominous modern rendering in the title page of Hobbes' *Leviathan*, where the social totality is 'personated' and embodied in the figure of a giant man, the sovereign who contains a multitude inside his body. Hobbes' collective figure, like Gormley's, seems to rise out of the earth, but *Field* has no unitary, integral, sovereign shape – except, of course, for the one that is given to it by the beholder. The spectator's body plays the role of Hobbes' Leviathan, insofar as the spectator frames the mass assembly in some subjective gestalt (a narrative or way of 'seeing as'). The closest Gormley comes to the totalitarian overtones of Leviathan as collective giant is his *Brick Man* (1987), which resonates both with the signs of collectivity (the bricks as the individuals in the social body) and the aura of the monolithic idol.

The combination of collective, local authorship and involvement, and the sheer visual power of the work, its rather demotic accessibility to many kinds of beholders and interpretations, make *Field* into

Total Strangers
1996
Cast iron
6 figures, 195 × 54 × 32 cm each
Installation, Kölnischer Kunstverein and adjacent street, Cologne, 1997

right, **Quantum Cloud III**
1999
Work in progress, the artist's
studio

opposite, **Quantum Cloud VII**
1999
Mild steel bar, 4 × 4 mm
224 × 144 × 114 m

one of the most successful public art projects of
its time. *Field* is not only for, but in a certain sense
of and by the masses, asserting the democracy
of artistic imagination and the possibility that the
sculptural 'genius of the place' might be formed
by its own inhabitants. Gormley serves, in that
case, more like a *gastarbeiter* than a visiting 'art
star', a guest-worker who assists in the process
of instituting a place.

His most recent large public works, *Angel of the
North* and *Quantum Cloud*, continue this process of
'outreach' beyond the boundaries of the cast body
and the conventional spaces of artistic exhibition.
The *Angel of the North* literally spreads its wings
in the highly traditional gesture of welcoming and
opening, combining what are by now the familiar
polarities of Gormley's work. The angel opens its
wings for flight, yet it stands firmly anchored
to resist winds of up to 100 miles per hour.
It combines an archaic rendering of the human

form with the modern, technical prostheses of
airplane wings. It expresses both the earth-
bound, gravitational pull of sculpture and its
transcendental, aerial, utopian idealism. Of all
Gormley's public works it is the one that has
sparked the most violent controversy, serving
as the focus of the usual battles over the waste
of public money on the arts. Villified for its size
(20 metres high, 54 metre wing span, 100 tons
of reinforced steel), its monumentality (some
critics associated it with Albert Speer and
fascist monuments); its expense; its danger as
a distraction to the 90,000 motorists who pass
it every day on the A1 road; its danger as a magnet
for lightning; and even its suggestion of a porno-
graphic image (one critic saw in it a flasher
opening his trenchcoat), the *Angel of the North*
has nonetheless rapidly achieved acceptance and
a kind of landmark status. Some works of public art
seem destined to undergo this kind of ritual of

Quantum Cloud
2000
Stainless steel bar
30 × 16 × 10 m
Bars, l. 1.5 m each

humiliation and sanctification. Maya Lin's Vietnam Veteran's Memorial is perhaps the most notable and moving example of this transformation from reviled to revered monument. Already it seems that the question about the *Angel of the North* is not 'What does it mean?', but 'How did it become a totem of this place?' Beyond the obvious resonance with the spread-eagled figure of the thunderbird often found on Native American totem poles, the *Angel of the North* expresses a resonance with its abandoned, post-industrial, wasteland site that helps to institute and resurrect it as place.

What will be the fate of *Quantum Cloud*, Gormley's latest project? An intricate assemblage of square steel tubes welded at precisely determined angles, this work flaunts its status as a technical, engineering marvel, as if it were the interior skeleton of a Modernist skyscraper caught at the moment of shattering. And yet hidden within this futuristic storm of steel is the vague silhouette of the totemic, monumental human form, a figure whose relation to any conceivable 'ground' has been rendered perfectly indeterminate, dispersed in a kind of aureole that reminds us of the radiant field around sacred icons.

The site and scale of *Quantum Cloud* will put it in competition with Nelson's Column, Westminster Bridge, Big Ben and other London landmarks. Will this be taken as an image of the digitized, cybernetic body, abstracted into a cloud of 'quanta' or bits of materialized information? Will it be taken as a totemic figure of what critic Tom Nairn has called 'the breakup of Britain' – Albion deconstructed?[31] If it is like Gormley's other public pieces, it will both invite and frustrate allegories of this kind, serving as a demotic invitation to enter a place for thought in the heart of urban distraction. As a continuation of Gormley's effort to 'think with materials' and with the sculpted body, it expresses his current tendency to move beyond his own body. The visual impression, in fact, is that of the body breaking up and dispersing in a cloud of steel segments (one could also read this, of course, as an image of convergence, as if the segments were like giant iron filings coalescing around the magnetic field left by an absent, almost invisible body). Once again the body is a place, but this time one whose boundaries are indeterminate, exploding or imploding, expanding or contracting. Perhaps that perfect shape for sculpture, the bomb, has 'gone off' in this work.

If one believes in linear, progressive narratives of artistic careers, one might conclude that *Quantum Cloud* signals the end of Gormley's entrapment in his own body and the beginning of a new phase in which the body, the human figure and the traditional sculptural choices of casting and carving have been replaced by or refunctioned as construction and assembly. The welded totems of David Smith and the entire Constructivist tradition in sculpture might be hovering about this cluster of steel tubes. But Gormley has already been 'out of his body' for over a decade and, more importantly, the story to be told about his work is not so much a matter of what he wants, but what sculpture seems to want from him. The general answer seems clear: Gormley's sculpture wants a place to be and to be a place. Where and in what form this desire will be gratified remains to be seen.

top, **Quantum Cloud II**
1999
Mild steel bar, 4 × 4 mm
234 × 270 × 109 cm

above, **Quantum Cloud XVI**
2000
Stainless steel bar, 5 × 5 mm
248 × 175 × 160 cm

Quantum Cloud XII (Crouching
Suspension)
1999
Mild steel bar, 4 × 4 mm
94 × 85 × 113 cm

1   Giorgio Vasari, *Lives of the Artists* (1568), Penguin Books,

     London, 1965, p. 25

2   *Exodus*, Book 20, Verses 4-5, King James Bible (1611)

3   Giorgio Vasari, op. cit., p. 26

4   Ibid.

5   Antony Gormley, conversation with the author, 2000

6   Robert Morris, 'Notes on Sculpture I', *Artforum*, Vol 4, No 6,

     New York, February, 1966, p. 42

7   Michael Fried, 'Art and Objecthood', *Artforum*, Vol 5, New York,

     Summer, 1967

8   'Sculpture would not deal with space ... Sculpture would be the

     embodiment of places.' Martin Heidegger, 'Art and Space', trans.

     Charles Seibert, *Man and World I*, Harper & Row, New York,

     1973, pp. 3-5

9   Martin Heidegger, 'Art and Space', op. cit., p. 6

10   Ibid.

11   For further reflections on the question of desire and lack in

     representational forms see my essay, 'What Do Pictures Really

     Want?', *October*, No. 77, MIT Press, Cambridge, Massachusetts,

     Summer, 1996, pp. 71-82

12   I am concerned to avoid the kind of historicism (marked by the

     'post-' and the 'pre-' that reduces the history of an art or

     medium to two phases separated by a 'rupture' located in the

     period that happens to correspond to the historian's field of

     specialization. For more on this, see 'The Pictorial Turn', *Picture

     Theory*, University of Chicago Press, 1994, especially pp. 22-23

13   See Katherine Hayles, *How We Became Posthuman*, University of

     Chicago Press, 1999; See also Donna Haraway, 'A Cyborg

     Manifesto', *Simians, Cyborgs and Women*, Routledge, New York

     and London, 1991

14   Gormley has said that he likes 'the idea that the body is an

     integrity. That you accept it as an integrated system', a remark

     that seems directed against the notion of the body as an

     arbitrary construction or heterogeneous assemblage. See

     Gormley/Theweleit, Schleswig-Holsteinischer Kunstverein and

Kunsthalle zu Kiel, Germany, 1999, p. 89

15 See Judith Butler, *Bodies That Matter: On the Discursive Limits of Sex*, Routledge, New York and London, 1993

16 Ibid.

17 Ibid.

18 Ibid.

19 I put to the side for the moment a 'third way' that works by assembly and construction.

20 If we locate the Adam and Eve analogy at the intersection of gender and engendering, we would have to say that while Adam is the first man from the standpoint of gender, he is also mother of Eve from the standpoint of engendering. These ambiguities of gender and reproduction are made marvelously complex in films like the *Alien* trilogy, which render the alien as an egg-laying dragon queen who implants her hatchlings to 'gestate' in the bodies of men and women, or *Invasion of the Body Snatchers*, in which zombie-like 'pod people' are engendered by a process of vegetative transfer of vital fluids through vines and tendrils. See Klaus Theweleit on the uncanny resemblance between some of Gormley's sculpture and these deadly pods in *Gormley/Theweleit*, op. cit., pp. 59, 113

21 One reason the tradition of assembled or constructed sculpture (David Smith, Anthony Caro, Cubist and Surrealist sculpture) seems antithetical to Gormley's practice is that it almost inevitably produces a sense of gesture and syntax in the figure, making it a body that acts in space rather than simply 'being there', which is, I take it, Gormley's aim.

22 Gormley describes his casting process as 'putting on the clothes of the dead and then being cut out'. *Critical Mass*, Stadtraum Remise, Vienna, 1995, p. 157

23 See *Critical Mass*, op. cit., p. 162. See also my discussion of Morris' treatment of the 'case' as a general sculptural problem, and the specific issue of the bomb casing, in *Picture Theory*, op. cit., chapter 8

24 Stephen Bann, *Antony Gormley: Still Moving, Works 1975–1996*, Japan

Association of Art Museums, 1996, p. 132

25 I'm reminded here of the contrast between Bob Dylan and Bruce Springsteen's ways of relating to an audience. Springsteen is a constant whirlwind of energy, passion and insistence, reaching out directly to the audience. Dylan (far more effectively, in my view) almost seems indifferent to the presence of the audience, focused on some incommunicable relation to his own words and music. Perhaps this is what Michael Fried's categories of 'absorption' and 'theatricality' really come down to.

26 Gaston Bachelard, *The Poetics of Space* (1958), Beacon Press, Boston, 1994, chapter 8

27 See Stephen Bann's evocation of Friedrich's *Monk and the Sea* in 'The Raising of Lazarus', *Antony Gormley*, Malmö Konsthall, Sweden, 1993, p. 71

28 Antony Gormley, *Critical Mass*, op. cit.

29 Emile Durkheim, *The Elementary Forms of Religious Life* (1912), trans. Karen Fields, Free Press, New York, 1995

30 Comparisons have been drawn with the terracotta army of Xian, China, the thousand bodhisattvas in Kyoto, Japan, and (in a contemporary context) with the mass produced 'surrogates' of Allan McCollum and the 'ranks of humanoid shells' of Magdalena Abakanovics. See Caoimhin Mac Giolla Leith, 'A Place Where Thought Might Grow', *Antony Gormley: Field for the British Isles*, Oriel Mostyn, Llandudno, Wales, 1994, pp. 24-26

31 Tom Nairn, *The Break-up of Britain: Crisis and Neo-Nationalism*, New Left Books, London, 1977

Contents

Selected exhibitions and projects
1968-82

1968-71
Studies Archaeology, Anthropology and Art History,
Trinity College, Cambridge

1971-74
Travels through Turkey, Syria, Afghanistan, Pakistan,
India, Iraq, Iran and Sri Lanka. Studies Buddhist
meditation at monastries in India and Sri Lanka

1974-75
Studies, **Central School of Art**, London

1975-77
Studies, **Goldsmiths School of Art**, London

1977-79
Studies, **Slade School of Fine Art**, London

1979
'Slade Post-graduate Exhibition',
Slade School of Fine Art (group)

1980
'Nuova Immagine',
XVI Triennale, Palazzo della Triennale, Galleria del
disegno, Milan (group)
Cat., *Nuova Immagine*, Mazzotta, Milan, text Flavio
Caroli

1981
Serpentine Gallery, London (solo)

Whitechapel Art Gallery, London (solo)
Cat., *Antony Gormley*, Whitechapel Art Gallery, London,
text Jenni Lomax

'Objects and Sculpture',
Institute of Contemporary Arts, London; **Arnolfini
Gallery**, Bristol (group)
Cat., *Objects and Sculpture*, Institute of Contemporary
Arts, London; Arnolfini Gallery, Bristol, texts Lewis
Biggs, Iwona Blazwick, Sandy Nairne and interviews
with the artists

'British Sculpture in the 20th Century',
Whitechapel Art Gallery, London (group)
Cat., *British Sculpture in the 20th Century*, Whitechapel
Art Gallery, London, texts Sandy Nairne and Nicholas
Serota

Two Stones,
Commission installed, Ashford, Kent

1982
'Aperto '82',
XL Venice Biennale (group)
Cat., *Aperto '82*, Electra, Milan, texts Guiseppe Galasso
and Tommaso Trini

'Hayward Annual: British Drawing'
Hayward Gallery, London (group)
Cat., *Hayward Annual: British Drawing*, Hayward
Gallery, London, texts John Elderfield and Mark Francis

Sleeping Places, in progress, studio in Kings Cross Road 1974

Selected articles and interviews
1968-82

1980
Author unknown, 'Nuove Immagine', *Flash Art*, Milan,
Summer

1981

Cooke, Lynne, 'Antony Gormley at the Whitechapel',
Artscribe, No 29, London
Morgan, Stuart, 'Antony Gormley: Whitechapel
Gallery', *Artforum*, New York, Summer

Biggs, Lewis, 'Objects and Sculpture', *Arnolfini Review*,
Bristol, July
Feaver, William, 'An Air of Light Relief', *The Observer*,
London, 26 June
Francis, Mark, 'Objects and Sculpture', *Art Monthly*,
London, July/August
Roberts, John, 'Objects and Sculpture', *Artscribe*, No
30, London
Russell Taylor, John, 'Objects and Sculpture', *The
Times*, London, 26 June

Installation, Whitechapel Art Gallery, London, 1981

Author unknown, 'Singleton Sculpture Installation',
S.E. Art News, London, August

1982
Feaver, William, 'Bellyfull of Ballast', *The Observer*,
London

Selected exhibitions and projects
1982-84

'Objects and Figures: New Sculpture in Britain',
organized by the Scottish Arts Council, Edinburgh,
Fruitmarket Gallery, Edinburgh, toured to **John
Hansard Gallery**, Southampton (group)
Cat., *Objects and Figures: New Sculpture in Britain*,
Scottish Arts Council, Edinburgh, text Michael Newman

1983
'The Sculpture Show',
Hayward Gallery, London; **Serpentine Gallery**,
London (group)
Cat., *The Sculpture Show*, Hayward Gallery, London;
Serpentine Gallery, London, texts Kate Blacker, Fenella
Crichton, Paul De Monchaux, Nena Dimitrijevic, Stuart
Morgan, Deanna Petherbridge, Bryan Robertson and
Nicholas Wadley

'New Art',
Tate Gallery, London (group)
Cat., *New Art*, Tate Gallery, London, text Michael
Compton

Coracle Press, London (solo)

'Transformations: New Sculpture from Britain',
XVII Bienal de São Paulo
organized by the British Council, London, toured to
Museu de Arte Moderna, Rio de Janiero; **Museo de
Arte Moderno**, Mexico; **Fundacao Calouste
Gulbenkian**, Lisbon (group)
Cat., *Transformations: New Sculpture from Britain*, The
British Council, London, texts Lewis Biggs, Lynne
Cooke, Mark Francis, John McEwan , Stuart Morgan,
John Roberts and Nicholas Serota

Installation, Coracle Press, London, 1983

1984
'1984',
Camden Arts Centre, London (group)
Cat., *1984*, Camden Arts Centre, London, texts Zuleika
Dobson and artists' statements

Salvatore Ala Gallery, New York (solo)
Cat., *Antony Gormley*, Salvatore Ala Gallery, Milan; New
York, text Lynne Cooke

'An International Survey of Recent Painting and
Sculpture',
The Museum of Modern Art, New York (group)
Cat., *An International Survey of Recent Painting and
Sculpture*, The Museum of Modern Art, New York, text
Kynaston McShine

Riverside Studios, London; **Chapter**, Cardiff (solo)
Cat., *Antony Gormley, Drawings From the Mind's Eye*,
Riverside Studios, London; Chapter, Cardiff, no text

Selected articles and interviews
1982-84

Januszczak, Waldemar, 'The Pop, Skip and Junk
Merchants of Sculpture', *The Guardian*, London, 15
December
Vaisey, Marina, 'The Art of Any Old Iron', *The Sunday
Times*, London, 19 December

Cork, Richard, 'Back to Nature', *Evening Standard*,
London, 23 December

1983

Drawings, in progress, Frederick Street studio, London, 1982

Archer, Michael, 'Antony Gormley', *Flash Art*, Milan,
December

Serota, Nicholas, 'Transformations: New Sculpture
from Britain', *Artefactum*, Antwerp, February/March

Newman, Michael, 'Man's Place: Four Works', *Art &
Artists*, New York

1984

Levin, Kim, 'The Clone Zone', *The Village Voice*, New
York, 15 May
Biegler, Beth, 'Antony Gormley at Salvatore Ala', *The
East Village Eye*, New York, June
Moorman, Margaret, 'Antony Gormley: Salvatore Ala',
ARTnews, New York, September
Linker, Kate, 'Antony Gormley', *Artforum*, New York,
October

Berman, Arthur, 'Antony Gormley', *TNT*, London, 2
October
Feaver, William, 'Variations on a Body', *The Observer*,

**CAMDEN
ARTS CENTRE**

NINETEEN
EIGHTY-FOUR

AN EXHIBITION

1 JANUARY **1984** 29 JANUARY

Selected exhibitions and projects
1984-85

Selected articles and interviews
1984-85

London, 23 September
Januszczak, Waldemar, 'Going up Like a Lead Balloon',
The Guardian, London, 2 October
Kopecek, Paul, 'Antony Gormley', *Art Monthly*, London,
October
Miller, Sanda, 'Antony Gormley at Riverside', *Artscribe*,
No 49, London
Packer, William, 'Body Building Exercises the
Sculptor's Mind', *The Financial Times*, London, 25
September
Rowat, Ken, 'Chapter Shows', *The Guardian*, London, 19
December
Vaisey, Marina, 'Art & Counterpart', *The Sunday Times*,
London, 16 September

Installation, Riverside Studios, London, 1984

'The British Art Show',
City of Birmingham Museum; **Ikon Gallery**,
Birmingham; **Royal Scottish Academy**, Edinburgh;
Mappin Art Gallery, Sheffield; **Southampton City Art
Gallery** (group)
Cat., *The British Art Show*, Arts Council of Great Britain,
London; Orbis Publishing Ltd., London, texts Marjorie
Allthorpe-Guyton, et al.

Ducann, Charlotte, 'Interview with Antony Gormley',
World of Interiors, London, November

'Metaphor and/or Symbol',
National Gallery of Modern Art, Tokyo; **National
Museum of Art**, Osaka (group)
Cat., *Metaphor and/or Symbol*, National Gallery of
Modern Art, Tokyo, texts Kenji Adachi, et al.

Archer, Michael, 'Antony Gormley', *Flash Art*, Milan,
December

Dimitrijevic, Nena, 'Antony Gormley', *Flash Art*, Milan,
January
Kopecek, Paul, 'Antony Gormley Talking to Paul
Kopecek', *Aspects*, London, No 25, January
Newman, Michael, 'Discourse and Desire in British
Sculpture', *Flash Art*, Milan, January

1985
'The British Show',
organized by Art Gallery of New South Wales, Sydney
and The British Council, toured to **Art Gallery of
Western Australia**, Perth; **Art Gallery of New South
Wales**, Sydney; **Queensland Art Gallery**, Brisbane; **The
Exhibition Hall**, Melbourne; **National Art Gallery**,
Wellington, New Zealand (group)
Cat., *The British Show*, Art Gallery of New South Wales,
Sydney, texts Sandy Nairne, et al.

1985

Galerie Wittenbrink, Munich (solo)

Bluemler, Detelf, 'Munchen', *Kunstzeitschrift*, Cologne,
May
Muller, Dorothee, ' Schwebende Giftige Maner: Antony
Gormley in der Muncher Galerie Wittenbrink',
Suddeutsche Zeitung, Munich, June

Galleria Salvatore Ala, Milan (solo)

Conti, Vianna, 'Antony Gormley', *Artefactum*, Antwerp,
September/ October

Stadtisches Galerie, Regensburg; **Kunstverein**,
Frankfurt (solo)
Cat., *Antony Gormley*, Stadtische Galerie, Regensburg;
Kunstverein, Frankfurt, texts Veit Loers and Sandy
Nairne

Author unknown, 'Antony Gormley', *Frankfurter
Allegmeine Zeitung*, 17 August
Author unknown, 'Bleierner Gast im Steinernen Haus',
Frankfurter Neue Presse, 13 August
Author unknown, 'Figuren in Fadenkreuz', *ART das
Kunstmagazine*, Hamburg, September
Author unknown, 'Stille Skulpturen und skelettierter
Kreisel', *Frankfurter Allgemeine Zeitung*, 14 August
Author unknown, 'Weit Ausgeholt', *Suddeutsche
Zeitung*, No 168, Munich, July

ANTONY GORMLEY

STÄDTISCHE GALERIE REGENSBURG

Selected exhibitions and projects
1985-86

'Anniottanta',
Galleria Communale d'Arte Moderna, Bologna (group)
Cat., *Anniottanta*, Galleria Communale d'Arte Moderna, Bologna, text Lynne Cooke

'Drawings 1981-1985',
Salvatore Ala Gallery, New York (solo)
Cat., *Antony Gormley Drawings*, Salvatore Ala Gallery, Milan; New York, no text

'Nuove trame dell'arte',
Castello Colonna di Genazzano, Italy (group)
Cat., *Nuove trame dell'arte*, Castello Colonna di Genazzano, Italy, text Achille Bonito Oliva

'Three British Sculptors',
Neuburger Museum, State University of New York, Purchase (group)

1986
'Between Object and Image',
organized by Minesterio de Cultura and The British Council, toured to **Palacio de Velasquez**, Parque del Retiro, Madrid; **Centre Cultural de la Caixa de Pensions**, Barcelona; **Centro de Arte Moderna de Fundacao Gulbenkian**, Lisbon (group)
Cat., *Between Object and Image*, Minesterio de Cultura; The British Council, Barcelona, texts Julian Andrews, Lewis Biggs and Juan Muñoz

'Drawings',
Victoria Miro Gallery, London (solo)

'The Generic Figure',
Corcoran Gallery of Art, Washington, DC (group)
Cat., *The Generic Figure*, Corcoran Gallery of Art, Washington, DC, text Ned Rifkin

Salvatore Ala Gallery, New York (solo)

'Art and Alchemy',
XLII Venice Biennale (group)

'Prospect '86',
Kunstverein, Frankfurt (group)
Cat., *Prospect '86*, Kunstverein, Frankfurt, texts Peter Weiermair, et al.

Selected articles and interviews
1985-86

Pokorny, Rita, 'Using the Body As If It Was a Face', *NIKE*, No 9, Munich, July/August/September

Somaini, Luisa, 'Antony Gormley', *La Republica*, Milan, 10 May
Somaini, Luisa, 'I dieci corpi dello scultore buddhista', *La Republica*, Milan, 5 June

Antolini, Adriano, 'La Scultura? Ha Corpo', *Il Giornale*, Turin, 26 May
Author unknown, 'Antony Gormley', *Flash Art*, Milan, March
Conti, Vianni, 'Antony Gormley', *Artefactum*, Antwerp, September/October
Nerozzi, Barbara, 'L'esperienza dell'orizzonte', *Gran Bazaar*, Nos 8/9, Milan, August/September
Weinstein, Matthew, 'Antony Gormley', *Westuff*, Milan, No 2, September
Weskott, Hanne, 'Antony Gormley', *Kunstforum*, Cologne

Bickers, Patricia, 'When is Sculpture not a Sculpture?', *Aspects*, No 29, London
Author unknown, 'Monumentale Body-Art', *Passauer Neue Presse*, Passau, July
Higgins, Judith, 'Antony Gormley', *ARTnews*, New York, December

1986
Zaya, Octavio, 'Antony Gormley: El Otro de uno Mismo', *Culturas Diario 16*, Madrid, 26 October

Studio, Talfourd Road, London, 1986

Richard, Paul, 'Upbeat Creature Feature at the Corcoran', *The Washington Post*, Washington, DC, 5 March

Fisher, Jean, 'Antony Gormley', *Artforum*, New York, January
Levin, Kim, 'Chernobyl, Mon Amour', *The Village Voice*, New York, 24 June
Rochette, Anne; Saunders, Wade, 'Antony Gormley at Salvatore Ala', *Art in America*, New York, November

Installation, Salvatore Ala Gallery, New York, 1986

Badoni, Rudolph Kramer, 'Ein Arm Spielt auf gespaltenei', *Die Welt*, Frankfurt, 10 September
Merkle, Harry, 'Lau, Laut und Laokoom', *Taz Berlin*, 20 September

Selected exhibitions and projects
1986-87

'Vom Zeichnen: Aspekte der Zeichnung',
Kunstverein, Frankfurt; **Kunstverein**, Kassel;
Museum Moderner Kunst, Vienna (group)
Cat., *Vom Zeichnen: Aspekte der Zeichnung*,
Kunstverein, Frankfurt, Kunstverein, Kassel; Museum
Moderner Kunst, Vienna, text Peter Weiermair

1987
'State of the Art',
Institute of Contemporary Arts, London (touring
exhibition) (group)
Cat., *State of the Art*, Chatto & Windus, London, texts
Sandy Nairne, Geoff Dunlop and John Wyver

'Antony Gormley: Five Works',
Serpentine Gallery, London (solo)
Cat., *Antony Gormley: Five Works*, Serpentine Gallery,
London; Arts Council of Great Britain, London, text
Antony Gormley

'Vehicle',
Salvatore Ala Gallery, New York (solo)

Galerie Hufkens de Lathuy, Brussels (solo)

'Chaos and Order in the Soul',
University Psychiatric Clinic, Mainz, Germany (group)
Cat., *Chaos and Order in the Soul*, University Psychiatric
Clinic, Mainz, Germany, text Peter Weiermair

'Avant-Garde in the Eighties',
Los Angeles County Museum of Art (group)
Cat., *Avant-Garde in the Eighties*, Los Angeles County
Museum of Art, text Howard N. Fox

'TSWA 3D',
City Walls, Derry, Ireland (group)
Cat., *TSWA 3D*, Institute of Contemporary Arts, London,
texts Tony Foster, Jonathan Harvey and James
Lingwood

'The Reemergent Figure',
Storm King Art Center, Mountainville, New York
(group)
Cat., *The Reemergent Figure*, Storm King Art Center,
Mountainville, New York, texts Suzi Gablik and Peter
Stern

'Documenta 8',
Kassel, Germany (group)
Cat., *Documenta 8*, Weber & Weidemeyer GmbH,
Kassel, text Manfred Snackenburger

'Mitographie: Luoghi Visibili/Invisibile dell'Arte',
Pinacoteca Comunale, Ravenna (group)
Cat., *Mitographie: Luoghi Visibili/Invisibile dell'Arte*,
Pinacoteca Comunale, Ravenna, texts Eugenio Battisti,
Bruno Bondini, Claudio Cerritale and Gillo Dorfles

'Man Made Man',
La Criée Halle d'Art Contemporain, Rennes, France
(solo)

Selected articles and interviews
1986-87

Cork, Richard, 'In Situ', *The Listener*, London, 5 June
Dorfles, Gillo, 'Antony Gormley', *Italian Vogue*,
February/March

1987
Archer, Michael, 'State of the Art', *Artforum*, New York,
Summer

Cork, Richard, 'Figures of Everyman', *The Listener*,
London, 19 March
Kent, Sarah, 'In the Lead', *Time Out*, London, 11 March
Morley, Simon, 'Serpentine Gallery: Antony Gormley',
Artline, London, April

Author unkown, 'Les Hommes et les Objets de Antony
Gormley', *Libre Belgique*, Brussels , May

Volp, Rainer, 'Geheimnisse sind immer sperrig', *Kunst
und Kirche*, Darmstadt, February

Vehicle, in progress, Dunstable, England, 1987

Author unknown, 'Man of Iron', *Stroll*, Nos 4/5,
Winnipeg
Gooding, Mel, 'Seeing the Sites', *Art Monthly*, London,
July/August

Brenson, Michael, 'Images that Express Essential
Human Emotions', *The New York Times*, 26 July
Zimmer, William, 'Figurative Sculpture Makes Impact at
Storm King Art Center', *The New York Times*, 2 August

Bode, Peter M., 'Kraft Nach Kassel', *Vogue*, Munich,
June

Lemee, Jean-Philippe, 'Antony Gormley Man Made
Man', *Art Press*, Paris, No 119

Chromosome, in progress, 1987

ANTONY GORMLEY
"VEHICLE"

30 April–26 May 1987
Opening reception: 30 April, 6–8 pm

salvatore ala
32 west 20th new york 10011 tel 741 5344

Selected exhibitions and projects
1987-88

'Viewpoint',
Musées Royaux des Beaux-Arts de Belgique, Brussels (group)
Cat., *Viewpoint*, Musées Royaux des Beaux-Arts de Belgique, Brussels, texts Marjorie Allthorpe-Guyton, et al.

Out of the Dark,
Commission installed, Martinsplatz, Kassel, Germany

'Drawings',
Seibu Contemporary Art Gallery, Tokyo (solo)
Cat., *Gormley*, Seibu Department Stores, Tokyo, text Michael Newman

1988
Burnett Miller Gallery, Los Angeles (solo)

'The Impossible Self',
Winnipeg Art Gallery, Manitoba; **Vancouver Art Gallery**, British Columbia (group)
Cat., *The Impossible Self*, Winnipeg Art Gallery, Manitoba, texts Bruce Ferguson, Antony Gormley, Sandy Nairne, et al.

'Starlit Waters: British Sculpture An International Art 1968-1988',
Tate Gallery Liverpool (group)
Cat., *Starlit Waters: British Sculpture An International Art 1968-1988*, Tate Gallery Liverpool, texts Lewis Biggs, Iain Chambers, Lynne Cooke, Richard Francis, Charles Harrison and Martin Kunz

'Rosc '88',
Guinness Hop Store, Dublin (group)
Cat., *Rosc '88*, Guinness Hop Store, Dublin, texts Aidan Dunne, Olle Granath and Patrick Murphy

'British Now: Sculpture et Autres Dessins',
Musée d'Art Contemporain de Montreal, (group)
Cat., *British Now: Sculpture et Autres Dessins*, Musée d'Art Contemporain de Montreal, texts Michel Brisebois and Sandra Grant Marchand

Contemporary Sculpture Centre, Tokyo (solo)
Cat., *Antony Gormley*, Contemporary Sculpture Centre, Tokyo, text Tadayasu Sakai

'Made to Measure',
Kettles Yard, Cambridge (group)
Cat., *Made to Measure*, Kettles Yard, Cambridge, text Hilary Gresty

'The Holbeck Sculpture',
Leeds City Art Gallery (solo)

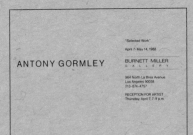

ANTONY GORMLEY — BURNETT MILLER GALLERY

'Selected Work'
April 7-May 14, 1988

964 North La Brea Avenue
Los Angeles 90038
213-874-4757
RECEPTION FOR ARTIST
Thursday April 7, 7-9 p.m.

JOHN BLAKE
ALIGHIERO BOETTI
SCOTT BURTON
ANTHONY CARO
RICHARD DEACON
HAMISH FULTON
ANTHONY GORMLEY
JASPER JOHNS
BRUCE NAUMAN
DAVID WARD
RICHARD WILSON
16 JULY
28 AUGUST
KETTLE'S YARD
GALLERY
MADE TO MEASURE

Selected articles and interviews
1987-88

De Ruyck, Jo, 'Verrassende verscheidenheid van de hedendaagse Britse kunst', *Het Volk*, Brussels, 17 December
Meuris, Jacques, 'Une saison britannique à points de vue multiples', *Libre Belgique*, Brussels, 26 December

Author unknown, 'Der Eiserne Gormley', *Frankfurter Rundschau*, Frankfurt, 29 January 1992
Author unknown, 'Kunst in der Stadt', *Kassel Kulturell*, September
Author unknown, 'Kunst soll anstoßen, nicht beruhigen', *Stadt Kassel*, 6 May
Schwarze, Dirk, 'Kunst in der Stadt', *Stadt Kassel*, 6 May

Graham-Dixon, Andrew, 'Antony Gormley's Bizarre Sculptural Techniques', *Harpers and Queen*, London, February
Levin, Kim, *The Village Voice*, New York, 20-26 May
Roustayi, Mina, 'An Interview with Antony Gormley', *Arts Magazine*, New York, September

1988

Enright, Robert, 'Inverse Aesthetics', *Border Crossings*, Manitoba, Summer

Pulson, Diana, 'Here's a Toast to Two Gents and, er, Sliced Bread?', *The Echo*, Liverpool, 24 May

Mays, John Bentley, 'British Sculpture Show Positive Step for MAC', *The Globe and Mail*, Montreal, 24 September

Warner, Marina, 'Statue of Liberty', *The Independent*, London, 4 May 1987

Sculpture for Derry Walls, in progress, Tay-Forth Foundry, Stirling, Scotland, 1987

Studio, 1988

Selected exhibitions and projects
1988-89

Brick Man,
commission for Leeds City Council, not realized

Out of the Dark, in progress, Lennox Foundry, Kent, 1989

1989
Museum of Modern Art, Louisiana, Humlebaek,
Denmark (solo)
Cat., *Antony Gormley*, Museum of Modern Art,
Louisiana, Humlebaek, Denmark, texts by Richard
Calvocoressi and Oystein Hjort

'It's a Still Life',
South Bank Centre, London (group)
Cat., *It's a Still Life*, South Bank Centre, London, text
Roger Malbert

Salvatore Ala Gallery, New York (solo)

Installation, Salvatore Ala Gallery, New York, 1989

Scottish National Gallery of Modern Art,
Edinburgh (solo)

'A Field for the Art Gallery of New South Wales, A Room
for the Great Australian Desert',
Art Gallery of New South Wales, Sydney, Australia
(solo)
Cat., *A Field for the Art Gallery of New South Wales, A
Room for the Great Australian Desert*, Art Gallery of New
South Wales, Sydney, texts Anthony Bond and Antony
Gormley

'Drawings',
McQuarrie Gallery, Sydney, Australia (solo)

Selected articles and interviews
1988-89

Author unknown, 'Brick Man', *The Sunday Telegraph*,
London, 13 November
Author unknown, 'Dropping a Brick', *Yorkshire Evening
Post*, Leeds, October
Bailey, Martin, 'Monumental Man Set to Tower Over
City', *The Observer*, London, 16 October
Bakewell, Joan, 'Vote to Cement History', *The Sunday
Times*, London, 30 October
Januszczak, Waldemar, 'The Might Have Been Man', *The
Guardian*, London, 17 December
Topp, Amanda, 'Brickman a Landmark', *Yorkshire
Evening Post*, Leeds, 18 August
Waterhouse, Keith, 'The Brick Colossus', *The Daily Mail*,
London, 1 September
Waugh, Auberon, 'Auberon Waugh's Column', *The
Sunday Telegraph*, London, 4 September
Williams, Alan, 'Permission to Stand', *The
Independent*, London, 4 July

1989
Christiansen, Flemming, 'Kroppe af bly', *Politiken*,
Copenhagen, 20 January
Kobke Sutton, Gertrud, 'Kroppens tyste tale',
Information, Denmark, 14 February
Meyer, Peter S., 'Suveraen iscenesaettelse', *Kristeligt
Dagsblad*, Denmark, 25 January
Wachtmeister, Marika, *Sysvenenska Dagbladet*, Malmo,
Sweden, 30 January

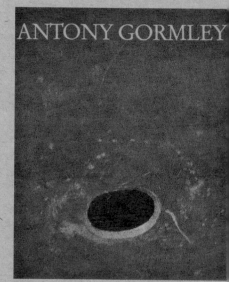

Catalogue cover, *Antony Gormley*, Museum of Modern Art, Louisiana,
Humlebaek, 1989

Brenson, Michael, 'A Sculptor Who Really Gets into His
Work', *The New York Times*, 17 May
Faust, Gretchen, 'New York in Review', *Arts Magazine*,
New York, September
Kaufman, Jason Edward, 'Antony Gormley's Human
Cyphers', *The New York Tribune*, 10 May
Reeves, Jennifer W., 'Cast in the Sculptor's Own
Mould', *The Christian Science Monitor*, New York, 14
August

Graham-Dixon, Andrew, 'Life Set Upon a Cast', *The
Independent*, London, 9 May
Henry, Clare, 'Figured Out: a Way of Lifting Base Metal
to Artistic Heights', *Glasgow Herald*, 26 May
MacDonald, Murdo, 'Body Language That Reflects the
Universal Condition', *The Scotsman*, Edinburgh, 11 May
Prince, Geraldine, 'A Cast of One', *The List*, Edinburgh,
18 May
Prince, Geraldine, 'A Plastered Sculptor', *The
Independent*, London, 2 May

Lynn, Elwyn, 'The Ambiguity of Intimacy', *The Weekend
Australian*, Sydney, 18-19 November
MacDonald, John, 'Sumptuous Commodities', *The
Sydney Morning Herald*, 18 November

Field for the Art Gallery of New South Wales, in progress, Sydney, 1989

Lynn, Elwyn, 'Subtly Reduced, with Abandon', *Weekend
Australian*, Sydney, 4-5 November

Selected exhibitions and projects
1989-91

'Objects of Thought',
Tornberg Gallery, Malmo, Sweden

'Visualization on Paper: Drawing as a Primary Medium',
Germans van Eck, New York (group)

1990
'Baring Light',
Burnett Miller Gallery, Los Angeles (solo)

'Drawing',
Burnett Miller Gallery, Los Angeles (solo)

'Great Britain – USSR',
The House of the Artist, Kiev; **The Central House of the Artist**, Moscow (group)
Cat., *Great Britain – USSR*, The House of the Artist, Kiev; The Central House of the Artist, Moscow, texts David Thorp and Jonathan Watkins

'British Art Now: A Subjective View',
organized by the British Council, toured to **Setagaya Museum**, Tokyo; **Fukuoka Art Museum**; **Nagoya City Museum**; **Tochigi Prefectural Museum of Fine Arts**; **Hyogo Prefectural Museum**; **Hiroshima City Museum** (group)
Cat., *British Art Now: A Subjective View*, The British Council, texts Andrew Graham-Dixon, Akio Obigane and Junichi Shioda

1991
'Drawings and Etchings',
Frith Street Gallery, London (solo)

'Field',
Salvatore Ala Gallery, New York (solo)

Galerie Christine et Isy Brachot, Brussels (solo)

'Places with a Past: Spoleto Festival USA',
Charleston, South Carolina (group)
Cat., *Places with a Past: Spoleto Festival USA*, Rizzoli International, New York, texts Mary Jane Jacob, John McWilliams, Nigel Redden and Theodore Rosengarten

'Inheritance and Transformation',
Irish Museum of Modern Art, Dublin (group)
Cat., *Inheritance and Transformation*, Irish Museum of Modern Art, Dublin, texts John Hutchinson and Declan McGonagle

Selected articles and interviews
1989-91

Wachtmeister, Marika, *Sysveneriska Dagbladet*, Malmo, Sweden, 30 January

Author unknown, 'Antony Gormley', *Art and Design*, Vol 5, No 3/4, London
Lynn, Victoria, 'Earth Above Ground', *Art & Text*, Sydney, Summer
Morley, Simon, 'Antony Gormley', *Tema Celeste*, Milan, April/June
Turnbull, Clive, 'Antony Gormley: The Impossible Self', *The Green Book*, Vol 3, No 1, Bristol

1990
Curtis, Cathy, 'Gormley's Vision', *Los Angeles Times*, 24 April
Pagel, David, 'Gormley', *Arts Magazine*, New York, April

1991
Graham-Dixon, Andrew, *The Independent*, London, 22 January

Brenson, Michael, 'Antony Gormley: Salvatore Ala Gallery', *The New York Times*, 29 March
Padon, Thomas, 'Antony Gormley: Salvatore Ala, New York', *Sculpture*, Washington, DC, September/October
Schwabsky, Barry, 'Antony Gormley', *Arts Magazine*, New York, Summer
Taplin, Robert, 'Antony Gormley at Salvatore Ala', *Art in America*, New York, November

Brenson, Michael, 'Visual Arts Join Spoleto Festival USA', *The New York Times*, 27 May
Danto, Arthur C., 'Spoleto Festival USA', *The Nation*, New York, 29 July

Learning to Think, in progress, workshop, Peckham, London, 1990

Flesh, in progress, studio, Peckham, London, 1990

GALERIE CHRISTINE ET ISY BRACHOT · RUE VILLA HERMOSA, 8 · 1000 BRUXELLES
TEL (32.2) 512.14.16 · FAX (32.2) 514.59.35

ANTONY GORMLEY

16.1 - 2.3.1991

Vernissage le mercredi 16 janvier de 19 à 21h
Opening woensdag 16 januari vanaf 19 tot 21 u

GALERIE CHRISTINE EN ISY BRACHOT · VILLA HERMOSASTRAAT, 8 · 1000 BRUSSEL
TEL (32.2) 512.14.16 · FAX (32.2) 514.59.35

Selected exhibitions and projects
1991-92

'Sculpture',
Galerie Nordenhake, Stockholm (solo)

'Field and Other Figures',
Modern Art Museum, Fort Worth,Texas ; **Centro Cultural/Arte Contemporaneo**, Mexico City; **San Diego Museum of Contemporary Art**, La Jolla, California; **Corcoran Gallery of Art**, Washington, DC; **Montreal Museum of Fine Arts** (solo)
Cat., *Antony Gormley: Field and Other Figures*, Modern Art Museum, Fort Worth, Texas, texts Richard Calvocoressi and Thomas McEvilley
Cat., *Antony Gormley: Field and Other Figures*, Montreal Museum of Fine Arts, texts Antony Gormley, Thomas McEvilley, Gabriel Orozco and Pierre Theberge

Field, in progress, San Diego Museum of Contemporary Art, 1992

'Colours of the Earth',
organized by the British Council, touring India and Malaysia (group)
Cat., *Colours of the Earth*, The British Council, texts Michael Casson, Alison Britton and Oliver Watson

'Sculpture',
Miller Nordenhake, Cologne (solo)

'Baring Light',
Gallery Shirakawa, Kyoto (solo)

1992
'Arte Amazonas',
Museu de Arte Moderna, Rio de Janiero, Brazil, toured to **Staatliche Kunsthalle**, Berlin; **Technische Sammlungen**, Dresden; **Ludwig Forum**, Aachen (group)
Cat., *Arte Amazonas*, Museu de Arte Moderna, Rio de Janiero; Goethe Institute, texts various authors

'Natural Order',
Tate Gallery Liverpool (group)
Cat., *Natural Order*, Tate Gallery Liverpool, text Penelope Curtis

'Recent Iron Works',
Burnett Miller Gallery, Los Angeles (solo)

'Learning to See: Body and Soul',
Contemporary Sculpture Centre, Tokyo (solo)
Cat., *Learning to See: Body and Soul*, Contemporary Sculpture Centre, Tokyo, text Antony Gormley, Masahiro Ushiroshoji

'C'est pas la fin du monde',

Selected articles and interviews
1991-92

Ericsson, Lars O., 'Klafsigt Malade traramar och blykroppar', *Dagens Nyheter*, Stockholm, 17 September
Harleman, Carl-Fredrick; van der Heeg, Erik, 'Concentrated Spaces', *Material Konst-Fanzine*, No 2, Stockholm
Sandquist, Gertrud, 'Manniskan som blykista', *Svenska dagbladet*, Stockholm, 14 September

Author unknown, 'Las Cosas ya Existen. La Escrultura ya Existe', *Poliester*, Mexico, March 1992
Burchard, Hank, 'Outstanding in his Field', *The Washington Post*, Washington, DC, 12 February 1993
Campo, Carlos, 'Un Cuerpo Colectivo Denominado Campo', *Activa*, Mexico, February 1992
Freudenheim, Susan, 'Contemplative Spectacle', *Los Angeles Times*, 17 October 1992
Grande, John K., 'Reviews: Montreal, Antony Gormley', *Artforum*, New York, October 1993
Hart, Jane, 'Interview with Antony Gormley', *Journal of Contemporary Art*, Vol 4, No 3, New York, Fall
McPherson, Anne, 'Reviews: Antony Gormley, Field', *Canadian Art*, Toronto, Winter 1993
Pincus, Robert L., 'Gormley's Engaging Vision of Humanity Takes Many Forms', *San Diego Union-Tribune*, 12 November 1992
Pincus, Robert L., 'Sculptor with Earthy World View', *San Diego Union Tribune*, 8 October 1992
Richard, Paul, 'The Field: It Figures', *The Washington Post*, Washington, DC, 8 March 1993
Tibol, Raquel, 'Edgar Negret y Antony Gormley en Mexico', *Proceso 801*, Mexico, 9 March 1992

1992
Metken, Gunter, 'Traver und Risse im Atelier der Tropen', *Frankfurter Allgemeiner Zeitung*, Frankfurt, 10 March

Pagel, David, 'Gormley's Sculptures Get Physical', *Los Angeles Times*, 8 October

Selected exhibitions and projects
1992-93

La Criée Halle d'Art Contemporain, Rennes; **Faux Mouvement**, Metz; **FRAC Basse Normandie**, Caen; **FRAC Poitou Charentes**, Angouleme (group)
Cat., *C'est pas la fin du monde*, La Criée Halle d'Art Contemporain, Rennes, texts Craig Owens, et al.

1993
Iron: Man,
Commission installed, Victoria Square, Birmingham

'The Human Factor: Figurative Sculpture Reconsidered',
Albuquerque Museum, New Mexico (group)
Cat., *The Human Factor*, Albuquerque Museum, New Mexico, text Christopher French

'Learning to See',
Galerie Thaddaeus Ropac, Paris (solo)
Cat., *Learning to See*, Thaddaeus Ropac, Paris; Salzburg, texts by Roger Bevan, Antony Gormley and Yehuda Safran

'Ha-Ha: Contemporary British Art in an 18th Century Garden',
Killerton Park, Exeter (group)
Cat., *Ha-Ha: Contemporary British Art in an 18th Century Garden*, Plymouth Polytechnic, texts Iwona Blazwick and Peter Pay

'The Raw and the Cooked',
Barbican Art Gallery, London; **Museum of Modern Art**, Oxford; **Glynn Vivian Art Gallery**, Swansea; **The Shigaraki Ceramic Cultural Park**, Japan (group)
Cat., *The Raw and the Cooked*, Museum of Modern Art, Oxford, texts Alison Britton and Martina Margetts

'The Body of Drawing',
Graves Art Gallery, Sheffield; **Mead Gallery**, University of Warwick; **Aberdeen Art Gallery**, Aberdeen; **Victoria Art Gallery**, Bath; **Oriel Mostyn**, Llandudno (group)
Cat., *The Body of Drawing*, Graves Art Gallery, Sheffield, texts Gerlinde Gabriel and Tony Godfrey

Konsthall Malmö, Sweden; **Tate Gallery Liverpool**; **Irish Museum of Modern Art**, Dublin (solo)
Cat., *Antony Gormley*, Konsthall Malmö, Sweden; Tate Gallery Liverpool; Irish Museum of Modern Art, Dublin, texts Stephen Bann, Lewis Biggs, Declan McGongle, Karsten Thjurfell

'European Field',
Centrum Sztuki Wspolczesnej, Warsaw; **Museum of Modern Art**, Ljubljana; **Muzej Suvremena Umjetnosti**, Zagreb; **Ludwig Museum**, Budapest; **Prague Castle**, Prague (solo)
Cat., *European Field*, Centrum Sztuki Wspolczesnej, Warsaw; Museum of Modern Art, Ljubljana; Muzej Suvremena Umjetnosti, Zagreb; Ludwig Museum Budapest, texts Stephen Bann, Antony Gormley, Marjetica Potrc and Marijon Susovski

European Field, in progress, Centrum Sztuki, Wspolczesnej, Warsaw , 1993

Selected articles and interviews
1992-93

1993
Grimley, Terry, 'Vision of Latest City Sculpture', *The Birmingham Post*, 14 September 1991
Grimley, Terry, 'Don't Knock This Bold Tribute to Our City's Past', *The Birmingham Post and Mail*, March

Delincee, Susanne, 'Koerper Formt Koerper', *Observer*, Vienna, 21 June

Lubbock, Tom, 'An Unnatural Device', *The Independent*, London, 13 July

Ericsson, Lars O., 'Kroppen som fodral for manniskans ide', *Dagens Nyheter*, Stockholm, 15 October
Lind, Maria, 'Fornimmandet finns i enfalden', *Material*, No 17, Stockholm
Wachtmeister, Marika, 'Kropper och dess holje', *Kristianstads-Bladet; Solvesborgs-Tidningen; Karlshamns Allehanda*, Sweden, 29 September
Zeylan, Hakan, 'Konsten angar oss alla', *Skanska Dagbladet*, Malmo, 8 October

Ayton, Ewa, 'Antony Gormley – Pole i inne rzezby', *Plastyka i Wychowanie*, Warsaw, July 1994
Blazevic, Dalibor, 'Ozivljavavje otudenih bica', *Gradski Vodic*, Croatia, June 1994
Glavan, Darko, 'M Mazemo biti biljka ili oblak', *Nedjeljna Dalmacija*, Croatia, 11 May 1994
Muzurovic, Lamija, 'Antony Gormley: Polja olovnih figura', *Kontura*, No 16, Zagreb, April
Vidovic, D., 'Krik za savjest covjecalistva', *Oslobocyeiye*, Sarajevo, 27 September 1994

Iron: Man, in progress, Victoria Square, Birmingham, 1993

Post, in progress, 'Ha-Ha', Killerton Park, Exeter, 1993

Selected exhibitions and projects
1993-94

'Field for the British Isles',
Tate Gallery Liverpool; **Irish Museum of Modern Art**,
Dublin; **Oriel Mostyn**, Llandudno; **Scottish National
Gallery of Modern Art**, Edinburgh; **Orchard Gallery**,
Derry; **Ikon Gallery**, Birmingham; **National Museum
of Wales**, Cardiff (solo)
Cat., *Field for the British Isles*, Oriel Mostyn,
Llandudno, texts Antony Gormley, Lewis Biggs, Adrian
Plant, Caoimhim Mac Giolla Leith, Marjetia Polvc

Galerie Nordenhake, Stockholm (solo)

Sound II,
Installed at Winchester Cathedral

1994
'Lost Subject',
White Cube, London (solo)

'Air and Angels' (with Alison Wilding),
ITN Building, London (solo)

'Open Space',
Commission for City of Rennes at La Place Jean-Monnet

'Sculptors' Drawings from the Weltkunst Collection',
Tate Gallery, London (group)

'From Beyond the Pale (Part 1)',
Irish Museum of Modern Art, Dublin (group)
Cat., *From Beyond the Pale*, Irish Museum of Modern
Art, Dublin, texts Brian Doherty, David Frankel, Edward
Kelly, Thomas McEvilley, Michael Tarantino, et al.

'The Essential Gesture',
Newport Harbor Art Museum, Newport Beach,
California (group)
Cat., *The Essential Gesture*, Newport Harbor Art
Museum, texts Michael Botwinick and Bruce Guenther

Lecture, Moderna Galerija, Ljubljana, Slovenia,
published in *M'ARS*, Vol 3/4,

'Turner Prize Shortlist',
Tate Gallery, London (group)

Sculptors' Drawings
Presented by the Weltkunst Foundation
5 July – 30 October 1994
Tate Gallery

Awarded Turner Prize, London

Selected articles and interviews
1993-94

Buck, Louisa, 'Feats of Clay', *GQ*, London, December
Clancy, Luke, 'Avoiding the Post-modern Trap', *The
Irish Times*, Dublin, 9 June
Clancy, Luke, 'Power of a Lapsed Optimist', *The Irish
Times*, Dublin, 30 April
Farrell, John, 'Gormley Show Has to Be Seen', *The
Sunday Press*, Dublin, 24 April
Feaver, William, 'Field Full of Folk and Banana Skins',
The Observer, London, 12 December
Lubbock, Tom, 'Fine Figures of a Man', *The
Independent*, London, 7 December
Side, Jeffrey, 'The Field as Metaphor', *Off the Cuff*,
University of Liverpool English Society, Lent 1994

Van der Heeg, Erik, 'Reviews: Antony Gormley:
Nordenhake, Stockholm', *Flash Art*, Milan, May/June
1994

l. to r., **Earth, End Product, Still Running, Body**,
in progress, Hargreaves Foundry, Halifax, 1993

Pietch, Hans, 'Er nimnt Mass on eigenen korper', *ART*,
Hamburg, March

1994
Norman, Geraldine, 'Sculptor Casts Himself in Star
Role', *The Independent*, London, 18 April
Dorment, Richard, 'Appearances can be Deceptive', *The
Daily Telegraph*, London, 6 April

Rankin-Reid, Jane, *Art & Text*, No 49, Sydney,
September

Hall, James, 'Frame Game', *The Guardian*, London, 7
November
Jiry, Louise; Hall, James, 'Bodymoulder Builds Big Lead
in Turner Prize Line-up', *The Guardian*, London, 20 July
Searle, Adrian, 'We Know You're in There', *The
Independent*, London, 4 November

Herbert, Susannah, 'Turner Prize for Sculptor Whose
Body Is His Art', *The Daily Telegraph*, London, 23
November
Greenburg, Sarah, 'Gormley Garners Turner', *ARTnews*,
New York, February

**The
Turner Prize
1994**

Selected exhibitions and projects
1994-95

'Testing a World View',
Tate Gallery Liverpool (solo)

Galeria Pedro Oliviera, Oporto, Portugal
(solo)
Cat., *Antony Gormley*, Noulso Galeria Pedro Oliviera,
Oporto, text Andrew Renton

'Artists' Impressions',
Kettle's Yard, Cambridge; **Castle Museum**,
Nottingham (group)
Cat., *Artists Impressions*, Kettle's Yard, Cambridge,
texts Sarah Glennie and Michael Harrison

1995
Book, *Antony Gormley*, Phaidon Press, London, texts
E.H. Gombrich, John Hutchinson, Antony Gormley,
Declan McGonagle, Lela B. Njatin

Angel of the North,
Commission for Gateshead Metropolitan Borough ,
Tyne and Wear

Broken Glass, Open Sky,
Commission installed, Ville de Rouen, France

Havmann,
Commission installed, Mo-i-Rana, Norway

Allotment I,
Commission installed, Herning Kunstmuseum,
Herning, Denmark

Kohji Ogura, Nagoya, Japan (solo)

'Critical Mass',
Stadtraum Remise, Vienna (solo)
Cat., *Critical Mass*, Stadtraum Remise, Vienna, texts
Edek Bartz, Antony Gormley and Andrew Renton

'Drawings',
Pace Foundation, San Antonio, Texas (solo)

'ARS 95',
Helsinki (group)
Cat., *ARS 95*, Nykytaiteen museo, Helsinki, texts Leevi
Haapala, Maria Hirvi and Maaretta Jaukkuri

Selected articles and interviews
1994-95

Cerveira Pinto, Antonio, 'O corpo pela Alma',
Independente, Lisbon, 9 December
Melo, Alexandre, 'O espaco do corpo', *Expresso*, Lisbon,
24 December

Ayton, Ena, 'I Am Fighting a Deconstructive World
View', *Art and Business*, Warsaw, March/April
Ball, Keith, 'Intimate Architecture – Antony Gormley',
Everything, No 13, London, April/May
Liiv, Toomas H, 'Antony Gormley teab vastust',
Puhapaevaleht, Tallinn, Estonia, 25 June
Wachtmeister, Marika, 'Mannen bakon blyholjina',
Femina, Stockholm, January

1995

Alberge, Dalya, 'A Towering Steel Angel Splits Town',
The Times, London, 7 February
Beckett, Andy, 'The Angel with A Dirty Face', *The
Independent on Sunday*, London, 28 July 1996
Pietsh, Hans, '"Engel des Nordens" mit 50 meter
Fluegelspann weite', *Art*, No 3, Hamburg, March 1996
Renton, Andrew, 'Antony Gormley: Reclaiming the
Subject or Making a Case for the Angel', *Art and Design
Profile*, No 41, London
Usherwood, Paul, 'A Wing and a Prayer', *Art Monthly*,
No 184, London, March
Whitley, John, 'Artist on the Side of the Angels', *The
Daily Telegraph*, London, 14 September 1996

Pedersen, Geir, 'Havmannen setters pa plass', *Rana
Blad*, Norway, 22 September

Stockinger, Andreas, 'Monumente, dauerhafter als
Erz', *Der Standard*, Vienna, 21/22 October
Sotriffer, Kristian, 'Von den Grundstellungen des
Menschenlebens', *Die Presse*, Vienna, 25 October

WHITE CUBE

Antony Gormley

Lost Subject

Open from
Friday 1 April until Saturday 7 May 1994

44 Duke Street
St. James's
London SW1Y 6DD
Tel: + 44 71 930 5373 Fax: + 44 71 930 9973
Open: Friday and Saturday 12-6pm or by appointment

Selected exhibitions and projects
1995-96

'The Weltkunst Collection: British Art of the 80s and 90s',
Irish Museum of Modern Art, Dublin (group)

'Here and Now',
Serpentine Gallery, London (group)

'Kwangju Biennale',
Kwangju, Korea (group)
Cat., *Kwangju Biennale*, Life and Dream Publishing,
Seoul, Korea, texts Oh Kwang-Su, et al.

'Glaube Hoffnung LiebeTod',
Kunsthalle, Vienna (group)
Cat., *Glaube Hoffnung LiebeTod*, Kunsthalle Wien;
Graphische Sammlung Albertina, Vienna, texts Patricia
Bickers, Harald Szeemann, et al.

1996
'New Work',
Obala Art Center, Sarajevo (solo)

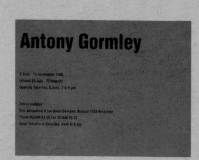

'Inside the Inside',
Galerie Xavier Hufkens, Brussels (solo)

'Outside the Outside',
Arts 04, St. Remy de Provence, France (solo)

'Still Moving: Works 1975-1996',
Museum of Modern Art, Kamakura, Japan, toured to
Nagoya City Art Museum, Aichi; **Takaoka Art
Museum**, Toyama; **Iwaki City Museum of Art**,
Fukushima; **Museum of Contemporary Art**, Sapporo;
Museum of Modern Art, Tokushima (solo)
Cat., *Still Moving: Works 1975-1996*, Japan Association
of Art Museums, Tokyo, texts Stephen Bann, Daniel
Birnbaum, Antony Gormley, Tadayasu Sakai and Kazuo
Yamawaki

'Field for the British Isles',
Hayward Gallery, London (solo)

'Body and Light and Other Drawings 1990-1994',
organized by Jay Jopling/White Cube, London
Independent Art Space, London (solo)
Cat., *Body and Light and Other Drawings 1990-1994*, Jay
Jopling/White Cube, London, no text

Selected articles and interviews
1995-96

Campbell-Johnston, Rachel, 'A Cut above the Rest', *The
Times*, London, 14 March

1996
Author unknown, 'Orijaska zeljezna konstrukcija',
Dnevni avaz, Sarajevo, 2 May
Author unknown, 'Promijenila se ideja o Zemlji ...',
Oslobodenje, Sarajevo, 2 May

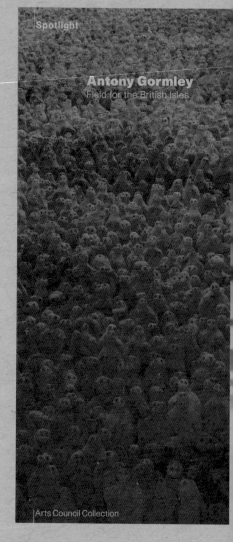

Cassim, Julia, 'Sculptures Cast an Enigmatic Silence',
Japan Times, Tokyo, 19 January 1997
Gormley, Antony; Nakamura, Hideki; Tanaka, Min,
'Interview with Antony Gormley/Hideki Nakamura/Min
Tanaka', *Revue de la pensee d'aujourd'hui*, Vol 25, No 2,
Tokyo, February 1997
Matsumoto, Hidetaka, *JAAM*, No 52, Japanese
Association of Art Museums, Tokyo, October 1997
Perron, Joel, 'Bodies Cloaked in Paradox', *Daily
Yomiuri*, Tokyo, 13 September

Cork, Richard, 'Critic's Choice of Autumn Shows', *The
Times*, London, 4 September
Cork, Richard, 'Full Frontal Power Show', *The Times*,
London, 24 September
Hilton, Tim, 'Portrait of the Young Man as an Artist',
The Independent on Sunday, London, 29 September
Jackson, Tina, 'The Galloping Gormley', *The Big Issue*,
London, 9 September
Kent, Sarah, 'Antony Gormley: Hayward', *Time Out*,
London, 25 September
Martin Gayford, 'A Tiny Tide Evokes the Vastness of
Humanity', *The Daily Telegraph*, London, 2 October
Sutcliffe, Thomas, 'Don't Dismiss the Craziness of
Modern Artists ...', *The Independent*, London, 5 October
Taylor, Annie, 'The Difference a Day Made', *The
Guardian*, London, 31 October

Selected exhibitions and projects

1996-97

'Works on Paper',
Irish Museum of Modern Art, Dublin, toured to
Ormeau Baths Gallery, Belfast (group)

'Un siècle de sculpture anglaise',
Galerie Nationale du Jeu de Paume, Paris (group)
Cat., *Un siècle de sculpture anglaise*, Galerie National
du Jeu de Paume, Paris, texts Stuart Morgan, Daniel
Abadie, Richard Cork, et al.

'Betong', (with Anish Kapoor and Miroslav Balka)
Malmö Konsthall, Sweden (group)
Cat., *Betong*, Malmö Konsthall, Sweden, texts Daniel
Birnbaum, Sune Nordgren, Ola Wedebrunn and Antony
Gormley

1997
Bearing IV,
Commission installed, Tongyoung City, Korea

'Total Strangers',
Kölnischer Kunstverein, Cologne (solo)
Cat., *Total Strangers*, Edition Cantz, Cologne, 1999,
texts Antony Gormley, Udo Kittelman, Ingrid Mehmel
and Antje von Graevenitz

'Our House',
Kunsthalle zu Kiel, Germany (solo)

'Another Place',
Cuxhaven, Germany (solo)
Cat., *Gormley/Theweleit*, Schleswig-Holsteinischer
Kunstverein; Cuxhavener Kunstverein, Germany, 1999,
texts Antony Gormley, Klaus Theweleit and Monika
Kubale-Theweleit

'Allotment',
Herning Museum, Denmark (solo)

'Bodyworks',
Kettle's Yard, Cambridge (group)
Cat., Kettle's Yard, Cambridge, text Michael Harrison

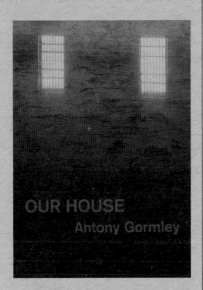

'L'empreinte',
Musée d'art Moderne, Centre Georges Pompidou, Paris
(group)
Cat., *L'empreinte*, Centre Georges Pompidou, Paris,
texts Georges Didi-Huberman and Didier Semin

'Material Culture',
Hayward Gallery, London (group)
Cat., *Material Culture*, Hayward Gallery, London; South
Bank Centre, London, texts Susan Ferleger Brades and
Greg Hilty

'Body',
Art Gallery of New South Wales, Sydney (group)
Cat., *Body*, Art Gallery of New South Wales, Sydney,
text Anthony Bond

Selected articles and interviews

1996-97

Lebovici, Elisabeth, 'Les Anglais sculptent leur
classicisme', *Libération*, Paris, 6 June

Birnbaum, Daniel, 'Betong med effekter', *Dagens
Nyheter*, Stockholm, 23 November
Ericsson, Lars O., 'Humanistisk arme invaderar
Magasin 3', *Dagens Nyheter*, Stockholm, 21 August
Magnusson, Erik, 'Hostens utstallningar raddade',
Sydsvenska Dagbladet, Malmö, 5 March 1997

Gormley, Antony; Gombrich, E.H., 'Gormley and
Gombrich in Conversation', *Prospect*, No 11, London,
August/September
Jackson, Tina, 'Go On - Make Your Mark', *The Big Issue*,
London, 16-29 December

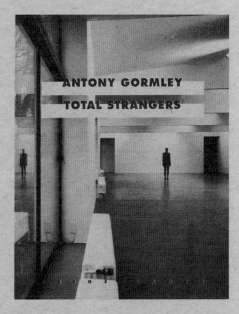

1997

Author unknown, 'Total Strangers', *Kölner Illustrierte*,
No 4, Cologne, April
Haase, Amine, 'Wer sind die Fremden?', *Kölner Stadt-
Anzeiger*, Cologne, 22-23 February

Ronnau, Jens, 'Antony Gormley: Our House: Kunsthalle
zu Kiel', *Artforum*, No 137, New York, June/August

Blomberg, Katja, 'Eisenmaenner auf ihrem Weg ins
Meer', *Frankfurter Allgemeine Zeitung*, Frankfurt am
Main, 18 September
Hohmeyer, Boris, 'Der Blick geht hin ueber nach
England', *Art*, Hamburg, November
Hartmann, Dora, 'Die Meditation der Kurgaste', *Taz
Bremen*, Kunstreisen, 18-19 October

Cork, Richard, 'Our Heavenly Bodies', *The Times*,
London, 25 February
Tromp, Ian, 'Bodyworks', *Sculpture*, Vol 16, No 3,
Washington, DC, March

Davila, Thierry, 'Empreinte, l'art cuelli sur le vif',
Beaux-Arts, France, April

Selected exhibitions and projects
1998-99

1998
Commission installed, *Angel of the North*, Gateshead, Tyne and Wear
Book, *Making an Angel*, Booth-Clibborn Editions, London, texts Gail-Nina Anderson, Stephanie Brown, Beatrix Campbell, Neil Carstairs, Antony Gormley and Iain Sinclair

Angel of the North, in progress, Hartlepool Steel Fabrications, Hartlepool

'Angel of the North',
The Gallery, Central Library, Gateshead (solo)

Rhizome,
Commission installed, Expo Parque, Lisbon
Cat., *Arte Urbana*, Expo '98, Lisbon, texts Alexandre Melo, Antonio Mega Ferreira, Joào Fernandes, et al.

'Critical Mass',
Royal Academy of Art, London (solo)
Cat., *Critical Mass*, Royal Academy of Art, London, texts George Benjamin and Antony Gormley

'Another Place',
Stavanger, Norway (solo)

'Force Fields',
Rupertinum, Salzburg, Austria (solo)

'Massens Ornament',
Kunsthallen Brandts Klaedefabrik, Odense, Denmark (group)
Cat., *Massens Ornament*, Kunsthallen Brandts Klaedefabrik, Odense, Denmark, texts by Siegfried Kracauer, Andreas Jurgensen and Carsten Thau

1999
'Insiders and Other Recent Work',
Galerie Xavier Hufkens, Brussels (solo)

'Intimate Relations',
MacClaren Art Centre, Barril, Ontario (solo)

'Intimate Relations',
Jablonka Galerie, Cologne (solo)

'Den Haag Sculptuur: British Sculpture of the Twentieth Century',
The Hague (group)
Cat., *Den Haag Sculptuur: British Sculpture of the Twentieth Century*, Fondation Het Voorhour de Beeldende Kunst, The Hague, texts W.J. Deetman and Norbert Lynton

Selected articles and interviews
1998-99

Buck, Louisa, *Moving Targets: A User's Guide to British Art Now*, Tate Gallery Publishing, London

Angel of the North, in progress, Hartlepool Steel Fabrications, Hartlepool

1998
Editorial, 'Angel of the North Spreads His Wings over Gateshead', *The Financial Times*, London, 16 February
Editorial, 'Brave Big Britannia', *The Times*, London, 16 February
Feaver, William, 'It Will Never Take Off ... ', *The Observer*, London, 22 February
Gayford, Martin, 'Is it a Bird? Is it a Plane?', *The Daily Telegraph*, London, 18 February
Grove, Valerie, 'Sculptor with Belief in His Guardian Angel', *The Times*, London, 21 February
Hetherington, Peter, 'On the Side of the Angel', *The Guardian*, London, 10 January
Searle, Adrian, 'Impressive Piece of Structural Design and Engineering', *The Guardian*, London, 17 February

Angel of the North in construction, Gateshead, Tyne and Wear

Stringer, Robin, 'Sculptor Faces the Critics and the Mass', *The Evening Standard*, London, 22 May
Thorpe, Vanessa, 'A Monumental Vision', *The Independent on Sunday*, London, 31 May
Bevan, Roger, 'Attraction of Opposites', *RA Magazine*, No 59, London, Summer

Borgen, Trond, 'En mystic stand', *Stavanger Aftenblad*, Stavanger, Norway, 9 June

Obrist, Hans Ulrich, 'Unbuilt Roads', *Contemporary Visual Arts*, No 20, London

1999

O'Brien, Peter, 'Middle of Somewhere', *National Post*, Toronto, 23 July

van Put, Roos, 'Antony Gormley en zijn rol op aarde', *Haagsche Courant*, The Hague, 21 June

Selected exhibitions and projects

1999–2000

'La Casa, Il Corpo, Il Cuore',
Museum Moderner Kunst Stiftung Ludwig Wien,
Vienna (group)
Cat., *La Casa, Il Corpo, Il Cuore*, Museum Moderner
Kunst Stiftung Ludwig Wien, Vienna, texts Lorand
Hegyi, Henry Meyric Hughes, et al.

'Reality and Desire',
Fundació Joan Miró, Barcelona (group)
Cat. *Reality and Desire*, Fundació Joan Miró, Barcelona,
texts Enrique Juncosa and Frederic Montornés

'At Home with Art',
Tate Gallery, London, and touring
Cat. *At Home with Art*, National Touring Exhibitions,
London, texts Susan Ferleger Brades and Colin Painter

'Presence: Figurative Art at the End of the Century',
Tate Gallery Liverpool (group)

2000
Commission installed, *Quantum Cloud*,
North Meadow Sculpture Project
Millennium Dome, Greenwich, London

'Field',
Vieille Église, Caumont, Picardy, France (solo)

'Strange Insiders',
fig-1, London (solo)

'Quantum Clouds and Other Work',
Galerie Thaddaeus Ropac, Paris (solo)
Cat., *Quantum Clouds and Other Work*, Galerie Thaddaeus
Ropac, Paris, texts Ann Hindry and Ian Tromp

Kwangju Biennale
Korea (group)
Cat., *Man + Space: Kwangju Biennale 2000*, Kwangju
Biennale Foundation, Korea, texts Oh Kwang-su, et al.

'Between Cinema and a Hard Place' (group)
Tate Modern, London

White Cube², London (solo)

Well,
Commission installed, Ministry of Health, Welfare and
Sport, The Hague

Passage,
Commission installed, Caumont, France

Site of Remembrance,
Commission installed, Oslo

Dorotheenblocke Haus 6,
Commission installed, Berlin

Mind-Body Column,
Commission installed, Osaka

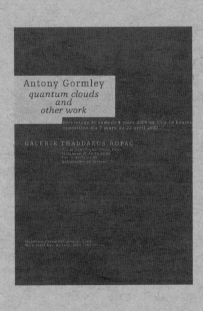

Selected reviews and interviews

1999–2000

2000
Searle, Adrian, 'He Created the Angel of the North.
Now He's Making an Even Bigger Millennium Man. But
Will it Stand Up?', *The Guardian*, London, 5 October
1999
Harlow, John, 'Angel of the South Heads for Clouds',
The Sunday Times, London, 12 December 1999
Cork, Richard, 'Meridian Messages Writ on Water', *The
Times*, London, 5 October 1999
Tromp, Ian, 'Body and Light: Antony Gormley's
Quantum Clouds', *Modern Painters*, London, Spring

Alberge, Dalya, 'A Towering Steel Angel Splits Town', *The Times*, London, 7 February, 1995

Allthorpe-Guyton, Marjorie, *Viewpoint*, Musées Royaux des Beaux-Arts de Belgique, Brussels, 1987

Anderson, Gail-Nina, *Making an Angel*, Booth-Clibborn Editions, London, 1998

Author unknown, 'Antony Gormley', *Art and Design*, Vol 5, Nos 3/4, London, 1989

Author unknown, 'Orijaska zeljezna konstrukcija', *Dnevni avaz*, Sarajevo, 2 May, 1996

Author unknown, 'Promijenila se ideja o Zemlji … ', *Oslobodenje*, Sarajevo, 2 May, 1996

Author unknown, 'Total Strangers', *Kölner Illustrierte*, No 4, Cologne, April, 1997

Bakewell, Joan, 'Vote to Cement History', *The Sunday Times*, London, 30 October, 1988

Ball, Keith, 'Intimate Architecture – Antony Gormley', *Everything*, No 13, London, April/May, 1994

Bann, Stephen, *Antony Gormley*, Konsthall Malmö, Sweden; Tate Gallery, Liverpool; Irish Museum of Modern Art, Dublin, 1993

Bann, Stephen, *European Field*, Centrum Sztuki Wspolczesnej, Warsaw; Muzej Suvremena Umjetnosti, Zagreb, 1993

Bann, Stephen, *Still Moving: Works 1975-1996*, Japan Association of Art Museums, Tokyo, 1996

Bartz, Edek, *Critical Mass*, Stadtraum Remise, Vienna, 1995

Beckett, Andy, 'The Angel with A Dirty Face', *The Independent on Sunday*, London, 28 July, 1996

Benjamin, George, *Critical Mass*, Royal Academy of Art, London, 1998

Bevan, Roger, 'Interview', *Learning to See*, Thaddaeus Ropac, Paris; Salzburg, 1993

Bevan, Roger, 'Attraction of Opposites', *RA Magazine*, No 59, London, Summer, 1998

Bickers, Patricia, 'When is Sculpture not a Sculpture?', *Aspects*, No 29, London, 1985

Biggs, Lewis, 'Objects and Sculpture', *Arnolfini Review*, Bristol, July, 1981

Biggs, Lewis, *Objects and Sculpture*, Institute of Contemporary Arts, London; Arnolfini Gallery, Bristol, 1981

Biggs, Lewis, *Antony Gormley*, Konsthall Malmö, Sweden; Tate Gallery, Liverpool; Irish Museum of Modern Art, Dublin, 1993

Birnbaum, Daniel, *Still Moving: Works 1975-1996*, Japan Association of Art Museums, Tokyo, 1996

Birnbaum, Daniel, 'Betong med effekter', *Dagens Nyheter*, Stockholm, 23 November, 1996

Blazwick, Iwona, *Objects and Sculpture*, Institute of Contemporary Arts, London; Arnolfini Gallery, Bristol, 1981

Blomberg, Katja, 'Eisenmaenner auf ihrem Weg ins Meer', *Frankfurter Allgemeine Zeitung*, Frankfurt, 18 September, 1997

Bluemler, Detelf, 'Munchen', *Kunstzeitschrift*, Munich, May, 1985

Bond, Anthony, *A Field for the Art Gallery of New South Wales, A Room for the Great Australian Desert*, Art Gallery of New South Wales, Sydney, 1989

Borgen, Trond, 'En mystic stand', *Stavanger Aftenblad*, Stavanger, Norway, 9 June

Brenson, Michael, 'Images that Express Essential Human Emotions', *The New York Times*, July, 1987

Brenson, Michael, 'Antony Gormley: Salvatore Ala Gallery', *The New York Times*, 29 March, 1991

Brenson, Michael, 'Visual Arts join Spoleto Festival USA', *The New York Times*, 27 May, 1991

Brown, Stephanie, *Making an Angel*, Booth-Clibborn Editions, London, 1998

Buck, Louisa, *Moving Targets: A User's Guide to British Art Now*, Tate Gallery Publishing, London, 1997

Calvocoressi, Richard, *Antony Gormley*, Museum of Modern Art, Louisiana, Humlebaek, Denmark, 1989

Calvocoressi, Richard, *Antony Gormley: Field and Other Figures*, Modern Art Museum, Fort Worth, Texas, 1991

Campbell, Beatrix, *Making an Angel*, Booth-Clibborn Editions, London, 1998

Campbell-Johnston, Rachel, 'A Cut above the Rest', *The Times*, London, 14 March, 1995

Campo, Carlos, 'Un Cuerpo Colectivo Denominado Campo', *Activa*, Mexico, February, 1992

Carstairs, Neil, *Making an Angel*, Booth-Clibborn Editions, London, 1998

Cassim, Julia, 'Sculptures Cast an Enigmatic Silence', *Japan Times*, Tokyo, 19 January, 1997

Cerveira Pinto, Antonio, 'O corpo pela Alma', *Independente*, Lisbon, 9 December, 1994

Clancy, Luke, 'Power of a Lapsed Optimist', *The Irish Times*, Dublin, 30 April, 1993

Clancy, Luke, 'Avoiding the Post-modern Trap', *The Irish Times*, Dublin, 9 June, 1993

Conti, Vianna, 'Antony Gormley', *Artefactum*, Belgium, September/October, 1985

Cooke, Lynne, 'Antony Gormley at the Whitechapel', *Artscribe*, No 29, London, 1981

Cooke, Lynne, *Antony Gormley*, Salvatore Ala Gallery, Milan, 1984

Cork, Richard, 'In Situ', *The Listener*, London, 5 June, 1986

Cork, Richard, 'Figures of Everyman', *The Listener*, London, 19 March, 1987

Cork, Richard, 'Critic's Choice of Autumn Shows', *The Times*, London, 4 September, 1996

Cork, Richard, 'Full Frontal Power Show', *The Times*, London, 24 September, 1996

Cork, Richard, 'Our Heavenly Bodies', *The Times*, London, 25 February, 1997

Cork, Richard, 'Meridian Messages Writ on Water', *The Times*, London, 5 October, 1999

Danto, Arthur C., 'Spoleto Festival USA', *The Nation*, New York, 29 July, 1991

De Ruyck, Jo, 'Verrassende verscheidenheid van de hedendaagse Britse kunst', *Het Volk*, Brussels, 17 December, 1987

Dimitrijevic, Nena, 'Antony Gormley', *Flash Art*, Milan, January, 1984

Dorment, Richard, 'Appearances can be Deceptive', *The Daily Telegraph*, London, 6 April, 1994

Editorial, 'Angel of the North Spreads His Wings over Gateshead', *The Financial Times*, London, 16 February, 1998

Editorial, 'Brave Big Britannia', *The Times*, London, 16 February, 1998

Ericsson, Lars O., 'Kläfsigt Malade traramar och blykroppar', *Dagens Nyheter*, Stockholm, 17 September, 1991

Ericsson, Lars O., 'Kroppen som fodral for manniskans ide', *Dagens Nyheter*, Stockholm, 15 October, 1993

Ericsson, Lars O., 'Humanistisk arme invaderar Magasin 3', *Dagens Nyheter*, Stockholm, 21 August, 1996

Feaver, William, 'It Will Never Take Off … ', *The Observer*, London, 22 February, 1998

Ferguson, Bruce, *The Impossible Self*, Winnipeg Art Gallery, Manitoba, 1988

Fisher, Jean, 'Antony Gormley', *Artforum*, New York, January, 1986

Foster, Tony, *TSWA 3D*, Institute of Contemporary Arts, London, 1987

Francis, Mark, 'Objects and Sculpture', *Art Monthly*, London, July/August, 1981

Gablik, Suzi, *The Reemergent Figure*, Storm King Art Center, Mountainville, New York, 1987

Gayford, Martin, 'Is it a Bird? Is it a Plane?', *The Daily Telegraph*, London, 18 February, 1998

Gombrich, E.H.; Gormley, Antony, 'Gormley and Gombrich in Conversation', *Prospect*, No 11, London, August/September, 1996

Gooding, Mel, 'Seeing the Sites', *Art Monthly*, London, July/August, 1987

Gormley, Antony, *The British Show*, Art Gallery of New South Wales, 1985

Gormley, Antony, *A Field for the Art Gallery of New South Wales, A Room for the Great Australian Desert*, Art Gallery of New South Wales, Sydney, 1989

Gormley, Antony, *Learning to See*, Thaddaeus Ropac, Paris; Salzburg, 1993

Gormley, Antony, *Critical Mass*, Stadtraum Remise, Vienna, 1995

Gormley, Antony, *Still Moving: Works 1975-1996*, Japan Association of Art Museums, Tokyo, 1996

Gormley, Antony; Gombrich, E.H., 'Gormley and Gombrich in Conversation', *Prospect*, No 11, London, August/September, 1996

Gormley, Antony, *Betong*, Malmö Konsthall, Sweden, 1996

Gormley, Antony; Nakamura, Hideki; Tanaka, Min, 'Interview with Antony Gormley/Hideki Nakamura/Min Tanaka', *Revue de la pensee d'aujourd'hui*, Vol 25, No 2, Tokyo, February, 1997

Gormley, Antony, *Critical Mass*, Royal Academy of Art, London, 1998

Gormley, Antony, *Making an Angel*, Booth-Clibborn Editions, London, 1998

Gormley, Antony, *Gormley/Theweleit*, Schleswig-Holsteinscher Kunstverein; Cuxhavener Kunstverein, Germany, 1999

Gormley, Antony, *Total Strangers*, Edition Cantz, Cologne, 1999

Graham-Dixon, Andrew, 'Antony Gormley's Bizarre Sculptural Techniques', *Harpers and Queen*, London, February, 1987

Graham-Dixon, Andrew, 'Life Set Upon a Cast', *The Independent*, London, 9 May, 1989

Grimley, Terry, 'Don't Knock this Bold Tribute to our City's Past', *The Birmingham Post and Mail*, March, 1993

Grove, Valérie, 'Sculptor with Belief in His Guardian Angel', *The Times*, London, 21 February, 1998

Haase, Amine, 'Wer sind die Fremden?', *Kölner Stadt-Anzeiger*, Cologne, 22/23 February, 1997

Hall, James; Jiry, Louise, 'Bodymoulder Builds Big Lead in Turner Prize Line-up', *The Guardian*, London, 20 July, 1994

Hall, James, 'Frame Game', *The Guardian*, London, 7 November, 1994

Harlow, John, 'Angel of the South Heads for Clouds', *The Sunday Times*, London, 12 December, 1999

Hart, Jane, 'Interview with Antony Gormley', *Journal of Contemporary Art*, Vol 4, No 3, New York, Fall, 1991

Harvey, Jonathan, *TSWA 3D*, Institute of Contemporary Arts, London, 1987

Hetherington, Peter, 'On the Side of the Angel', *The Guardian*, London, 10 January, 1998

Higgins, Judith, 'Antony Gormley', *ARTnews*, New York, December, 1985

Hilton, Tim, 'Portrait of the Young Man as an Artist', *The Independent on Sunday*, London, 29 September, 1996

Hindry, Ann, *Quantum Clouds and Other Work*, Galerie Thaddaeus Ropac, Paris, 2000

Hjort, Oystein, *Antony Gormley*, Museum of Modern Art, Louisiana, Humlebaek, Denmark, 1989

Jackson, Tina, 'The Galloping Gormley', *The Big Issue*, London, 9 September, 1996

Jackson, Tina, 'Go On - Make Your Mark', *The Big Issue*, London, 16-29 December, 1996

Jacob, Mary Jane, *Places with a Past*, Rizzoli International, New York, 1991

Jiry, Louise; Hall, James, 'Bodymoulder Builds Big Lead in Turner Prize Line-up', *The Guardian*, London, 20 July, 1994

Kaufman, Jason Edward, 'Antony Gormley's Human Cyphers', *The New York Tribune*, 10 May, 1989

Kent, Sarah, 'In the Lead', *Time Out*, London, 11 March, 1987

Kent, Sarah, 'Antony Gormley: Hayward', *Time Out*, London, 25 September, 1996

Kittelman, Udo, *Total Strangers*, Edition Cantz, Cologne, 1999

Kobke Sutton, Gertrud, 'Kroppens tyste tale', *Information*, Denmark, 14 February, 1989

Kopecek, Paul, 'Antony Gormley', *Art Monthly*, London, October, 1984

Kubale-Theweleit, Monika, *Gormley/Theweleit*, Schleswig-Holsteinischer Kunstverein; Cuxhavener Kunstverein, Germany, 1999

Lemee, Jean-Philippe, 'Antony Gormley Man Made Man', *Art Press*, No 119, Paris, 1987

Levin, Kim, 'The Clone Zone', *The Village Voice*, New York, 15 May, 1984

Levin, Kim, 'Chernobyl, Mon Amour', *The Village Voice*, New York, 24 June, 1986

Lind, Maria, 'Fornimmandet finns i enfalden', *Material*, No 17, Stockholm, 1993

Liiv, Toomas H, 'Antony Gormley teab vastust', *Puhapaevaleht*, Tallinn, Estonia, 25 June, 1994

Lingwood, James, *TSWA 3D*, Institute of Contemporary Arts, London, 1987

Linker, Kate, 'Antony Gormley', *Artforum*, New York, October, 1984

Loers, Veit, 'Antony Gormley', Stadtische Galerie Regensburg, Frankfurter Kunstverein, 1985

Lubbock, Tom, 'An Unnatural Device', *The Independent*, London, 13 July, 1993

Lubbock, Tom, 'Fine Figures of a Man', *The Independent*, London, 7 December, 1993

Lynn, Victoria, 'Earth Above Ground', *Art & Text*, Sydney, Summer, 1989

McEvilley, Thomas, *Antony Gormley: Field and Other Figures*, Modern Art Museum, Fort Worth, Texas, 1991

McPherson, Anne, 'Reviews: Antony Gormley, Field', *Canadian Art*, Toronto, Winter, 1993

McWilliams, John, *Places with a Past*, Rizzoli International, New York, 1991

Magnusson, Erik, 'Hostens utstallningar raddade', *Sydsvenska Dagbladet*, Malmö, 5 March, 1997

Martin Gayford, 'A Tiny Tide Evokes the Vastness of Humanity', *The Daily Telegraph*, London, 2 October, 1996

Matsumoto, Hidetaka, *JAAM*, No 52, Japanese Association of Art Museums, Tokyo, October, 1997

Mehmel, Ingrid, *Total Strangers*, Edition Cantz, Cologne, 1999

Melo, Alexandre, 'O espaco do corpo', *Expresso*, Lisbon, 24 December 1994

Miller, Sanda, 'Antony Gormley at Riverside', *Artscribe*, No 49, London, 1984

Moorman, Margaret, 'Antony Gormley; Salvatore Ala', *ARTnews*, New York, September, 1984

Morgan, Stuart, 'Antony Gormley, Whitechapel Gallery', *Artforum*, New York, Summer, 1981

Morley, Simon, 'Serpentine Gallery: Antony Gormley', *Artline*, London, April, 1987

Morley, Simon, 'Antony Gormley', *Tema Celeste*, Siracusa, April/June, 1989

Muzurovic, Lamija, 'Antony Gormley: Polja olovnih figura', *Kontura*, No 16, Zagreb, April, 1993

Nairne, Sandy, *Objects and Sculpture*, Institute of Contemporary Arts, London; Arnolfini Gallery, Bristol, 1981

Nairne, Sandy, *British Sculpture in the 20th Century*, Whitechapel Art Gallery, London, 1981

Nairne, Sandy, *Antony Gormley*, Stadtische Galerie Regensburg, Frankfurter Kunstverein, 1985

Nairne, Sandy, *The British Show*, Art Gallery of New South Wales, Sydney, 1985

Nairne, Sandy, *State of the Art*, Channel 4, London, 1987

Nairne, Sandy, *The Impossible Self*, Winnipeg Art Gallery, Manitoba, 1988

Newman, Michael, *Objects and Figures: New Sculpture in Britain*, The Scottish Arts Council, Edinburgh, 1982

Newman, Michael, 'Discourse and Desire in British Sculpture', *Flash Art*, Milan, January, 1984

Newman, Michael, *Gormley*, The Seibu Department Stores, Tokyo, 1987

O'Brien, Peter, 'Middle of Somewhere', *National Post*, Toronto, 23 July, 1999

Obrist, Hans Ulrich, 'Unbuilt Roads', *Contemporary Visual Arts*, No 20, London, 1998

Orozco, Gabriel, *Antony Gormley: Field and Other Figures*, Modern Art Museum, Fort Worth, Texas, 1989

Padon, Thomas, 'Antony Gormley: Salvatore Ala, New York', *Sculpture*, Washington, DC, September/October, 1991

Pagel, David, 'Antony Gormley', *Arts Magazine*, New York, April, 1990

Pedersen, Geir, 'Havmannen setters pa plass', *Rana Blad*, Norway, 22 September, 1995

Perron, Joel, 'Bodies Cloaked in Paradox', *Daily Yomiuri*, Tokyo, 13 September, 1996

Pietch, Hans, 'Er nimmt Mass on eigenen korper', *ART*, Hamburg, March, 1993

Pietsh, Hans, '"Engel des Nordens" mit 50 meter Fluegelspann weite', *ART*, Hamburg, March, 1996

Plant, Adrian, *Field for the British Isles*, Oriel Mostyn, Llandudno, 1994

Pokorny, Rita, 'Using the Body As If It Was a Face', *Neue Kunst in Europe*, No 9, Munich, July/August/ September, 1985

Potrc, Marjetica, *European Field*, Museum of Modern Art, Ljubljana, 1993

Rankin-Reid, Jane, *Art & Text*, No 49, Sydney, September, 1994

Redden, Nigel, *Places with a Past*, Rizzoli Internationsl, New York, 1991

Renton, Andrew, *Critical Mass*, Stadtraum Remise, Vienna, 1995

Renton, Andrew, 'Antony Gormley: Reclaiming the Subject or Making a Case for the Angel', *Art and Design Profile*, No 41, London, 1995

Roberts, John, 'Objects and Sculpture', *Artscribe*, No 30, London, 1981

Rochette, Anne; Saunders, Wade, 'Antony Gormley at Salvatore Ala', *Art in America*, New York, November, 1986

Ronnau, Jens, 'Antony Gormley: Our House: Kunsthalle zu Kiel', *Artforum*, No 137, New York, June/August, 1997

Rosengarten, Theodore, *Places with a Past*, Rizzoli Internationsl, New York, 1991

Roustayi, Mina, 'An Interview with Antony Gormley', *Arts Magazine*, New York, September, 1987

Safran, Yehuda, *Learning to See*, Thaddaeus Ropac, Paris; Salzburg, 1993

Sakai, Tadayasu, *Antony Gormley*, Contemporary Sculpture Centre, Tokyo, 1988

Sakai, Tadayasu, *Still Moving: Works 1975-1996*, Japan Association of Art Museums, Tokyo, 1996

Sandquist, Gertrud, 'Manniskan som blykista', *Svenska dagbladet*, Stockholm, 14 September, 1991

Saunders, Wade; Rochette, Anne, 'Antony Gormley at Salvatore Ala', *Art in America*, New York, November, 1986

Schwabsky, Barry, 'Antony Gormley', *Arts Magazine*, New York, Summer, 1991

Searle, Adrian, 'Impressive Piece of Structural Design and Engineering', *The Guardian*, London, 17 February, 1998

Searle, Adrian, 'He Created the Angel of the North. Now He's Making an Even Bigger Millennium Man. But Will it Stand Up?', *The Guardian*, London, 5 October, 1999

Serota, Nicholas, *British Sculpture in the 20th Century*, Whitechapel Art Gallery, London, 1981

Serota, Nicholas, 'Transformations: New Sculpture from Britain', *Artefactum*, Antwerp, February/March, 1983

Side, Jeffrey, 'The Field as Metaphor', *Off the Cuff*, University of Liverpool English Society, Lent, 1994

Sinclair, Iain, *Making an Angel*, Booth-Clibborn Editions, London, 1998

Snackenburger, Manfred, *Documenta 8*, Weber & Weidemeyer GmbH, Kassel, 1987

Sotriffer, Kristian, 'Von den Grundstellungen des Menschenlebens', *Die Presse*, Vienna, 25 October, 1995

Stern, Peter, *The Reemergent Figure*, Storm King Art Center, Mountainville, New York, 1987

Stockinger, Andreas, 'Monumente, dauerhafter als Erz', *Der Standard*, Vienna, 21/22 October, 1995

Stringer, Robin, 'Sculptor Faces the Critics and the Mass', *The Evening Standard*, London, 22 May, 1998

Susovski, Marijon, *European Field*, Muzej Suvremena Umjetnosti, Zagreb, 1993

Sutcliffe, Thomas, 'Don't Dismiss the Craziness of Modern Artists ...', *The Independent*, London, 5 October, 1996

Taplin, Robert, 'Antony Gormley at Salvatore Ala', *Art in America*, New York, November, 1991

Taylor, Annie, 'The Difference a Day Made', *The Guardian*, London, 31 October, 1996

Theberge, Pierre, *Antony Gormley: Field and Other Figures*, Modern Art Museum, Fort Worth, Texas, 1989

Theweleit, Klaus, *Gormley/Theweleit*, Schleswig-Holsteinscher Kunstverein; Cuxhavener Kunstverein, Germany, 1999

Thorpe, Vanessa, 'A Monumental Vision', *The Independent on Sunday*, London, 31 May, 1998

Tibol, Raquel, 'Edgar Negret y Antony Gormley en Mexico', *Proceso 801*, Mexico, 9 March, 1992

Tromp, Ian, 'Bodyworks', *Sculpture*, Vol 16, No 3, Washington, DC, March, 1997

Tromp, Ian, 'Body and Light: Antony Gormley's Quantum Clouds', *Modern Painters*, London, Spring, 2000

Tromp, Ian, *Quantum Clouds and Other Work*, Galerie Thaddaeus Ropac, Paris, 2000

Turnbull, Clive, 'Antony Gormley: The Impossible Self', *The Green Book*, Vol 3, No 1, Bristol, 1989

Usherwood, Paul, 'A Wing and a Prayer', *Art Monthly*, No 184, London, March, 1995

Ushiroshoji, Masahiro, *Antony Gormley: Learning to See: Body and Soul*, Contemporary Sculpture Centre, Tokyo, 1992

Van der Heeg, Erik, 'Reviews: Antony Gormley: Nordenhake, Stockholm', *Flash Art*, Milan, May/June, 1994

von Graevenitz, Antje, *Total Strangers*, Edition Cantz, Cologne, 1999

Warr, Tracey; Jones, Amelia, *The Artist's Body*, Phaidon Press, London, 2000

Weiermair, Peter, *Vom Zeichnen: Aspekte der Zeichnung*, Frankfurter Kunstverein; Kasseler Kunstverein; Museum Moderner Kunst, Vienna, 1986

Weiermair, Peter, *Chaos and Order in the Soul*, University Psychiatric Clinic, Mainz, Germany, 1987

Weinstein, Matthew, 'Antony Gormley', *Westuff*, No 2, September, 1985

Weskott, Hanne, 'Antony Gormley', *Kunstforum*, Cologne, 1985

Whitley, John, 'Artist on the Side of the Angels', *The Daily Telegraph*, London, 14 September, 1996

Wyver, John, *State of the Art*, Channel 4, London, 1987

Yamawaki, Kazuo, *Still Moving: Works 1975-1996*, Japan Association of Art Museums, Tokyo, 1996